Being-Black-in-the-World

Being-Black-in-the-World

N. Chabani Manganyi

WITS UNIVERSITY PRESS

Published in South Africa by:
Wits University Press
1 Jan Smuts Avenue
Johannesburg 2001

www.witspress.co.za

First published 1973 by Spro-Cas/Ravan Press

Wits University Press edition 2019

The publishers gratefully acknowledge permission from African Sun Media
to republish the afterword, which first appeared in Ndebele, S.N. 'Being-black-
in-the-world and the future of blackness', *The Effects of Race*, edited by Nina
G. Jablonski and Gerhard Maré. Stellenbosch: African Sun Media, 2018,
pp. 89–105.

http://dx.doi.org.10.18772/12019093689

978-1-77614-368-9 (Paperback)
978-1-77614-369-6 (Web PDF)
978-1-77614-370-2 (EPUB)
978-1-77614-371-9 (Mobi)

Project manager: Simon Chislett
Copyeditor: Danya Ristić
Proofreader: Lee Smith
Cover designer: Hybrid Creative
Typesetter: MPS
Typeset in 10.5 point Crimson

Contents

Foreword

Writing a foreword to a seminal text that is being re-published in a different historical moment demands acute sensitivity and a delicate balance. On the one hand, there is the need to be faithful to the authorial voice and preserve the essence of the original text. On the other hand, it is also important to ensure that the text is appropriately framed and located, with perspicacity, for a new generation of readers, even though the authorial voice and textual content originated in a different temporal moment.

This was the task confronting Grahame Hayes, Roshan Cader and myself, as an editorial collective working on the re-publication of N. Chabanyi Manganyi's *Being-Black-in-the-World*, which was first published in the turbulent political period of 1973. Four primary coordinates propelled and guided an approach to this project. First, many of us as scholars in the arts, humanities and social sciences had been re-engaging with Manganyi's work over several years because we believed him to have been an undervalued critical black intellectual and scholar in South Africa. Many of us were committed to having him appropriately located and recognised within fields such as art, literature, psychology, political science, anthropology and so on.

Second, since 2015 South Africa's political landscape had seen a groundswell of calls for decolonising universities, curricula, social institutions, notions of science and art, and a recalibration of what constitutes the canon across most disciplines. The synergies between Manganyi's *Being-Black-in-the-World* and these decolonising calls for an interrogation of the legacies of coloniality on forms of knowledge, subjectivity and power were patently clear, even though Manganyi was much less known as a public intellectual in comparison to the likes of eminent figures such as Stephen Bantu Biko. Third, this particular iteration of the *decolonial turn* in South Africa had prompted a re-reading of key black intellectuals such as Aimé Césaire, Frantz Fanon, Biko and, to a different degree, Manganyi. While a number of writers had written about Manganyi's work in the contemporary moment (e.g. Boonzaier and Kessi, 2016), it is Njabulo S. Ndebele's (2018) instructive interpretive essay, '"Being-Black-in-the-World" and the Future of "Blackness"', that reveals the prescient nature of Manganyi's thinking in the 1970s. In my discussions with Grahame Hayes, he characterised Ndebele's essay as 'a timeous piece that is a marvellous demonstration of how to read *Being-Black-in-the-World* in 2019, that is simultaneously engaged, historical, critical, and yet preserves the essence of much of the 1973 original' (Stevens, 2019). Given the quintessential nature of this essay, it has been included as an afterword in this re-publication. Fourth, it is rare to have the opportunity to engage with an author more than four-and-a-half decades after he penned a seminal manuscript, and so we were intent on hearing Manganyi's own reflections on the text, its major influences, its intentions then and its potential meanings now. I have included reflections from my conversations with Manganyi, which took place at his home. Our conversations centred on his reflections on the background to writing the text, and what he thought of the complexities of the text re-circulating in a contemporary moment.

What this allowed for was a contemplation of how this text is located within Manganyi's oeuvre, its place within the historical context of its birthing and production, and the major influences that came to shape it. In addition, it offered us provocations about how well texts travel across time, space, histories and contexts, and the relevance of texts such as these to our contemporary world.

Manganyi's intellectual contributions have spanned almost five decades, within his home discipline of psychology, but also in literary studies, philosophy, education, history, politics, art and aesthetics. Some of his most notable texts include *Mashangu's Reverie and Other Essays* (1977); *Looking Through the Keyhole* (1981); *Political Violence and the Struggle in South Africa*, edited with André du Toit (1990); *Treachery and Innocence: Psychology and Racial Difference in South Africa* (1991); *On Becoming a Democracy: Transition and Transformation in South African Society* (2004); *Apartheid and the Making of a Black Psychologist: A Memoir* (2016); not to mention his biographies on Gerard Sekoto, Es'kia Mphahlele and Dumile Feni.

At the risk of presenting an oversimplified characterisation and periodisation of his oeuvre, it can nevertheless be said that Manganyi's work has traversed several genres. His earlier interests were clearly more clinically focused in relation to psychological understandings of embodiment, but increasingly these evolved into work on the body and its intersections with experiences of alienation within a racist world. Stories of alienation and existential crises also opened up the terrain of the life story genre in his writings, and these were gradually crystallised in fictionalised autobiographies, biographies and memoirs. While these developments were partly a result of specific disciplinary exposures that occurred at particular moments, they then signalled a move towards a more socially relevant psychology and, finally, also a fluid maturation and diversification of his ideas pertaining to people's experiences of their subjectivity in a racialised world.

Being-Black-in-the-World is an important text for a number of reasons: It reflects Manganyi's growing confidence in his own disciplinary knowledge and professional expertise at the time. It gestures towards a deliberate directional shift in his application of psychology to the social world and reveals coherence in his thinking about the relationship between black subjects and their existential experiences in the world. The text furthermore captures the 1970s' zeitgeist amongst many black South Africans, Africans and those in the African diaspora. Intellectually, it is also one of the earliest South African psychological texts that explicitly engages with debates about psychology's relevance. By this I mean that the text embraces the psychological dimensions of being a racialised social subject. It is preoccupied, too, with what is currently referred to as 'studies of the psychosocial' – studies that focus on the mutually reinforcing relationship between the individual and society, or, stated differently, the internal worlds of social subjects and the external material worlds that we inhabit. Furthermore, it is truly concerned with understanding the psyche-soma relationship within contexts of racialised inequality – that is, the ways in which the mind and body intersect when race persists as a significant social cleavage. Finally, it is an explicit exemplar of earlier intellectual genealogies that spoke to the importance of undoing hierarchies of knowledge, power and being through addressing the legacies of coloniality. As such, *Being-Black-in-the-World* is a cutting-edge text that at the time of its publication revealed certain convergences in Manganyi's intellectual trajectory, gestured towards the orientation of much of his future work and today reveals its enduring relevance to post-colonial societies.

The historical context of textual production is critical to note as that which partly shapes the nature and content of the text itself. *Being-Black-in-the-World* was produced in the decade following heightened forms of resistance to apartheid, as well as increased modes of repression. Key liberatory organisations such as the African National Congress and the Pan Africanist Congress were banned, and the state responded to events such as the Sharpeville anti-pass law protests by enacting draconian forms of subjugation. In addition, the book was published during the Durban Moment – a time in which Black Consciousness was hegemonic as a political strand and organised labour was gaining ground through trade union organisation. Central to this moment were the Durban strikes of 1973, during which black labour and broader anti-apartheid organisations operated together to highlight and protest the economic and socio-political plight of the South African black working class in particular.

In my conversations with Manganyi, he clearly felt that Biko's influence on the political moment was monu-mental, and *Being-Black-in-the-World* was a response to this pulse – a mode of protest, if you will. Manganyi suggested that as an alert scholar and black intellectual, one could not fail to be aware of Biko at the time, despite acknowledging that he had not directly engaged with Biko himself. In addition, it is apparent from the text, and other reflections from Manganyi, that he had been influenced by the writings of Fanon, by the philosophical work on Négritude by writers such as Léopold Sédar Senghor and Césaire, by the current of existentialism in philosophy and the social sciences, and by the psychoana-lytic conceptualisations of the relationship between the psyche (mind) and soma (body) – much of the latter of which could be described as the precursors of the embodiment and affect theory of the late twentieth and early twenty-first centuries.

Of course, despite these compelling arguments about the importance of this work, Manganyi himself raised various critical questions about its re-publication when we were initially considering it and discussing its form and function in contemporary South Africa. From the outset he interrogated the language of the text – whether it could be understood today, or was not perhaps a time capsule of sorts that was only applicable to the moment of textual production.[1] The issue that Manganyi was essentially raising was the extent to which, and how well, theory travels across time, space, context and histories. More importantly, when engaged with further on this he appeared to be reflecting on the linguistic constructions and the discursive repertoires that vary within the crafting of texts over time. He was concerned that the text's apparently robust tenor may be interpreted as overly combative in its register today, as he believed that it reflected a specific historical moment of social and political protest. He was also uncertain about whether the interpretations offered by the text would still be relevant today, and the extent to which the text would be a coherent elucidation of the contemporary context. While these are important questions, they may in part have indicated how Manganyi viewed the vastly different moments across his professional life. The early years of his career involved the production of this text, and one of the self-defined apex points of this career

---

[1] A note on the use of racial terms throughout this edition: Manganyi's writing is of a particular time and thus his use of racial categories reflects how race was discussed and these categories were used in that period. This re-publication maintains fidelity to Manganyi's original text and therefore retains his use of these terms.

was his contribution to the nation-building project within the post-apartheid Nelson Mandela administration, as director general of higher education. These differing contributions may have resulted in an anxiety that his earlier work may not find resonance in the current social and political imperatives central to the nation-building project.

Of course, re-reading and re-interpreting a seminal historical text is not simply a form of presentism in which one reads the past through the lens of the present, nor a form of revisionism in which one selectively re-writes history. In *Freud and the Non-European*, Edward Said notes in his dialogue with Jacqueline Rose and Christopher Bollas:

> [Historical writings are] further actualized and animated by emphases and inflections that [the author] was obviously unaware of, but that [their] writing permits. Thus later history reopens and challenges what seems to have been the finality of an earlier figure of thought, bringing it into contact with cultural, political and epistemological formations undreamed of by – albeit affiliated by historical circumstances with – its author. (2003: 25)

This allows an entirely new generation of readers to reflexively interpret the history, context, subjecthood, analytic logics and authorial intent embedded in the original text, in potentially infinite and novel ways. Under these circumstances, *Being-Black-in-the-World* has a legitimate place in the present as a lens through which to interpret contemporary South Africa. Furthermore, its consistent application across the same South African context and history, despite the temporal differences in production and present interpretation, makes such a contemporary reading of the text even more plausible.

More particularly, today *Being-Black-in-the-World* will be read at a time of deep crisis in the dominant liberal political project, when the left is attempting to recalibrate itself while there is a resurgence of right-wing conservatism and populism. Anti-immigrant sentiment, xenophobia, crude nationalisms, narrow ethnicisms and intense forms of racialisation have once again reared their heads (Stevens, 2018). Walter Mignolo (2019) suggests that this may be part and parcel of the new logics of liberalism and neo-liberalism today – a world in which there is the drive to increasingly incubate rudimentary forms of 'othering' as a means to differentiate and equalise the concentrations of power across competing systems of capital that now exist throughout a multipolar globe.

However, this is also the historical juncture at which new organic social movements are replacing the old mass-based politics of the twentieth century. These movements are attempting to tackle matters related to migration and transnationalism, racism and the historical effects of colonisation and coloniality. They are articulating a mode of politics that takes seriously the relationship between identities, subjectivities, bodies, affects, histories and materialities (Stevens, 2018). In South Africa, our histories of race and racism continue to have a significant valence within these debates and processes. *Being-Black-in-the-World* will no doubt find fertile ground for re-interpretation under these national, African and global conditions, and I suspect will be re-read with a fresh perspective by many who have already encountered Manganyi's work. I hope that it will also be voraciously studied by a new and engaged readership with an appetite for understanding the complex realities of our world today – that is, reading the concerns of the past as a way of illuminating and analysing their continuities in the present.

When asked how he believed the text would be received by interlocutors today, Manganyi simply stated that he hoped that it would be seen as an assertion and affirmation of the rights of all human beings – both black and white. As a text, its breadth and depth are quite remarkable, given how short it is in extent. Manganyi tackles matters of African ontology and epistemology, illuminates the metaphysics and phenomenology of being black and illustrates the existential effects of coloniality on the black psyche in particular. He asks crucial questions about what it means to be black and African, and whether these are essential categories or ways of being in the world. He engages with Black Consciousness as a form of identity politics that should be seen as a mode of solidarity and strategic essentialism rather than a form of racialism. He notes the continued delinking of psyches, bodies, communities and objects in a racialised world and the perverse relationships that such a world generates, ultimately producing existential vacuums that can only result in suffering. He reaffirms the importance of the humanity of all, and considers social change as a systemic, iterative and ongoing process.

For a new readership as well as those who have read Manganyi's *Being-Black-in-the-World* many years ago, it will become apparent why his work should be considered a national treasure. It will no doubt find its position within the histories of South African knowledge-production processes, where Manganyi himself will also take his rightful place as a scholar, theorist, engaged citizen and son of South Africa, Africa and the world.

Garth Stevens, Professor of Psychology,
University of the Witwatersrand
May 2019

References

Boonzaier, F. and Kessi, S. (eds.) (2016) *Psychology in Society*, 52, pp. 1–133.

Manganyi, N.C. (1977) *Mashangu's Reverie and Other Essays*. Johannesburg: Ravan Press.

Manganyi, N.C. (1981) *Looking Through the Keyhole: Dissenting Essays on the Black Experience*. Johannesburg: Ravan Press.

Manganyi, N.C. (1991) *Treachery and Innocence: Psychology and Racial Difference in South Africa*. Johannesburg: Ravan Press.

Manganyi, N.C. (ed.) (2004) *On Becoming a Democracy: Transition and Transformation in South African Society*. Pretoria: Unisa Press/Leiden: Koninklijke Brill NV.

Manganyi, N.C. (2016) *Apartheid and the Making of a Black Psychologist*. Johannesburg: Wits University Press.

Manganyi, N.C. and Du Toit, A. (eds.) (1990) *Political Violence and the Struggle in South Africa*. Johannesburg: Southern Book Publishers/London: Macmillan.

Mignolo, W. (2019) *Venezuela: The Symptoms of Multipolarity*. 29 January. https://doc-research.org/2019/01/venezue-la-symptoms-multipolarity/ (accessed 29 April 2019).

Ndebele, N. (2018) '"Being-Black-in-the-World" and the Future of "Blackness"', in Jablonski, N.G. and Maré, G. (eds.) *The Effects of Race*. Stellenbosch: African Sun Media, pp. 89–108.

Said, E. (2003) *Freud and the Non-European*. London: Verso.

Stevens, G. (2018) Raced Repetition: Perpetual Paralysis or Paradoxical Promise? *International Journal of Critical Diversity Studies*, 1 (2), pp. 42–57.

Stevens, G. (2019) Email communication with G. Hayes, 10 April.

Introduction

B*eing-Black-in-the-World* is intended as a contribution to the growing body of books and papers on the black experience. It is only very recently that concerted efforts have become manifest in the field of black studies at various universities in Africa and elsewhere. The extent of academic and lay interest in this field received concrete expression in the publication by Heinemann Educational Books in 1970 of a three-volume source book entitled *The African Experience*, which was edited by J.N. Paden and E.W. Soja.[1]

The efforts of these academics are definitely deserving of our guarded admiration, although it is probably true to say that the most important contribution on the black experience will have to come from Africa. For it is here, on the African continent, where the great and intricate drama of being-black-in-the-world is taking place. In a field of study and life where there have been so many self-proclaimed experts, it is not always possible to say much that is worth saying. It is partly for this reason that I

---

[1] John Paden, an international politics lecturer and African studies scholar, and Edward Soja, an urban geographer, were both based at Northwestern University, USA, at the time.

conceived of this book as essentially a small collection of essays reflecting my thinking on a number of subjects.

There has been no desire on my part to impose any form of structural unity on the book. To impose a structure would have been to tell an unpardonable lie, since my existence and experience are themselves fairly unstructured. The only formal structural requirements I attempted to adhere to are those relating to the internal consistency of the individual essays. This means that each essay has been an attempt to reflect on a specific aspect of the black experience. Overlapping with respect to theme reflects the writer's conviction that experience is not discrete but continuous.

This collection of essays addresses itself to a limited number of important questions. I consider the questions to be of general significance to South African society as a whole. Issues which are of such significance should be of interest to both academics and members of the lay public. It became necessary to keep this fact in view in the treatment of the various subjects in the collection. Technical terminology was reduced to a minimum in the more demanding essays. A glossary was considered necessary for purposes of clarity. Consideration of the collection as a whole revealed that there were enough questions raised for both the academically inclined and the general reader.

A question found throughout the book may be formulated as follows: Is there a black mode of being-in-the-world? Stated differently: Is being-black-in-the-world different in fundamental respects to being-white-in-the-world? Some specific essays deal particularly with this question; others are concerned with it in a more indirect fashion.

Of more general significance and interest are the essays on the urban Africans and communication, Black Consciousness, the meaning of change and the postscript on Prof. Engelbrecht's contribution on time and neuroses in Africans.[2] As I prepare this book, the city of Durban is in the grip of one of the worst strikes, by African workers, in the history of our land for a long time.[3] There is growing concern that the strikes may snow-ball into the other urban areas in the rest of the country. These strikes caught the country napping. One of the lessons which should be learnt from the Durban troubles is that the communication gap, like all the other famous gaps between whites and blacks, is widening into a gulf. Factors which militate against black–white communication in organisational settings are some of the concerns of the essay on the urban Africans.

The widening of the communication gap has other important implications, one of which relates to the question of change in South African society. When observers discuss this type of change, are they talking about goal-directed and structured change or other forms of unexpected change? Is change in South Africa equally meaningful to both blacks and

[2] Prof. Engelbrecht was a professor of philosophy at the University of the North in the 1970s. At the time, the university was an apartheid-created 'bush college' for Africans. Engelbrecht was also acting rector of the university at the time, and told the early South African Students' Organisation leaders 'Don't allow yourselves to be used by NUSAS [National Union of South African Students]; you are not instruments.' This sentiment was consistent with upholding the *separation* between blacks and whites that was the mainstay of apartheid policy.
[3] 'On 9 January 1973, workers at the Coronation Brick and Tile factory, outside Durban, came out on strike. Immediately thereafter, workers from small packaging, transport and ship repairs companies also came out on strike. By the end of March 1973, close on 100,000 mainly African workers, approximately half of the entire African workers employed in Durban, had come out on strike' (South African History Online, 2014). This strike wave was a turning point in the emergence of non-racial trade unions.

whites? At this stage in our history, it appears that it is necessary to put a spotlight on the meaning and significance of change. It should be appreciated that the problem of the meaning of change and its implications is crucial to future race relations in South Africa.

Appearing together with the communication gap between blacks and whites has been the assault on national cohesiveness, which is progressively being replaced by polarisation in attitudes, interests and goals. Part of this polarisation is a result of the policies of separate development while the other should be associated with the development of the philosophies of Black Consciousness and solidarity. Within the South African context, the words 'Black Consciousness and solidarity' have come to be invested with so much that may be regarded as emotional, either in the pronouncements of its proponents or in the defensive reactions of the white public. There appears to be a danger that this emotive quality may make slogans or clichés out of the philosophies of Black Consciousness and solidarity. This danger may only be averted if we look more closely at the meaning and significance of these philosophies within the South African context. My essay on Black Consciousness was conceived with the awareness that there is still probably a great deal of misunderstanding about Black Consciousness and solidarity as a posture both within the black communities and outside.

Racial stereotyping in South Africa is not dead. It has, for example, appeared very recently from the pen of a professor of philosophy at one of our black universities. This academic has used very respectable (erudite) language to say that Africans live in a time of their own. This time, according to him, is different from natural time (white time). He arrives at the curious conclusion that this consideration should be used to justify separate development. The postscript on time and neuroses in this collection concerns itself briefly with the views of Prof. Engelbrecht on this matter.

Let me return to the other essays which deal with the issue of being-black-in-the world more specifically. Within our country, there are people representing different racial groups, languages, religions and cultures. In race-conscious environments, interest groups organised along racial lines often develop as they have in South Africa. The plural nature of our society, for example, is often referred to, but only in so far as it acts as a justification for a rigid white–black demarcation. 'Us and Them' concerns itself with this question of racial group identity and the related one of the differences in modes (patterns) of being-in-the-world between blacks and whites. 'Us' and 'them' in our environment are 'primary' words, in Buber's (1958) sense,[4] of relating and distancing; they refer to the in-group and the out-group. These primary forms of relating between blacks and whites are shown to be associated with differences in the way blacks and whites relate to their bodies, to other people, to objects and to time. 'Us' and 'them' are expressive of an attitude – the attitude of considering an individual as being within one's group or outside it.

'Being-black-in-the-world' is concerned with the controversy surrounding the concept 'African personality'. There have, broadly, been two usages of this concept. The first usage is one that is generally adopted by white observers who have attempted to use the concept as a psychological construct. A second usage

---

[4] Martin Buber (1878–1965) was an existentialist philosopher whose book, *I and Thou* (first published in German in 1923, and in English in 1937), and its philosophy of dialogue, has greatly influenced generations of critical thinkers.

is one which could be said to understand the concept as refer-
ring to a lifestyle. Understood in this way, the concept becomes
interchangeable with Senghor's concept 'Négritude'. This usage is
commonly adopted by some blacks. We consider the controversy
which has been going on to have been completely unnecessary,
for reasons which are stated in the relevant section of this book.

'Nausea' raises the question of whether the experience of
suffering and meaninglessness (absurdity), sometimes so characteristic of life, is of the same order for both blacks and whites.[5]
People in despair often ask the question, 'Why?' Is this question
of the same order for blacks and for whites? If there should be
black and white modes of being-in-the-world, the answers to
these questions are likely to be different for the two existential
experiences.

The 'Reflections' cover a number of related issues, chiefly in
the area of mental health. These reflections arise mainly from my
experience as a clinical psychologist. It seems to me that we need
to begin to interest ourselves in the psychiatric (mental health)
side of our life as South Africans. We have been telling all and
sundry that we are capable of teaching the world something novel
about racial harmony and peaceful coexistence in a multiracial
(multinational?) society. Perhaps it is time for us to turn inward
and assess whether our claims are not in excess of our progress.
One way of monitoring this progress appears to be an evaluation
of psychiatric morbidity – the study of the extent to which our
society is integrative, in the sense of promoting and supporting

---

[5] *Nausea* (first published in French in 1938, and in English in 1949) is the title of
a novel by Jean-Paul Sartre (1905–1980), and is an important concept in existential thought. However, in chapter 5 ('Nausea'), Manganyi refers to another
existential writer, Albert Camus (1913–1960), when talking about nausea, and
not Sartre.

individual and community psychic health. The laboratories for such studies are there in South Africa's black communities. It is true to say that in these communities the highest cumulative unfavourable social experiences are to be found. These are populations at special risk, from a mental health point of view.

I would like to make a few more general remarks. These remarks amount to a position statement which may help clarify my preoccupation with the body. This preoccupation is not morbid, but arises out of the recognition of the body's central position in existence. We make our approaches to the world through our bodies: The body is movement inwards and outwards. To what extent does the body determine the experience of being-black-in-the-world or being-white-in-the-world? This is a crucial question. It may be answered briefly at this stage. An individual develops a personalised, idiomatic mental (image) concept of his body. This is what I describe as the *individual schema*. If he should be black, like myself, he begins to know, through various subtle ways, that his black body is unwholesome, that the white body is the societal standard of wholesomeness. This later development in body awareness I describe as the *sociological schema*. Each one of us lives with two schemas – cooperative or at odds with each other. These two body schemas (images), I believe, have a lot to do with the experiences of being-black-in-the-world and being-white-in-the-world.

Some of the ideas expressed in this book are decidedly provocative. There have been no malicious intentions of the kind usually associated with political propaganda. As I see it, my contribution will have been significant if it should generate informed debate by black scholars and others on the ideas expressed in this collection.

1 | Who Are the Urban Africans?

The problem of effective communication in commerce and industry is not unique to the South African situation. Even in countries with fairly homogenous populations and long histories of industrialisation and urbanisation, this problem continues to constitute a thorny issue for industrial psychologists and communication specialists. This fact in itself is a very clear index of the complexity of the problem.

In the case of South Africa, the complexity of the communication process is compounded by our singular history and the existence of an intricate politico-economic structure. This problem cannot but be complex, since South Africa's economy must continue to move in the direction of economic integration (multiracialism) while politically moving more in the direction of multinationalism (separate development). This unhappy marriage between the economy and political or ideological demands is leading to a surfacing of a developing debate. The local press has carried a number of articles relating to whether Africans should become members of organised labour (trade unions) or not. This debate appears to be related to a growing fear of possible future labour unrest. This concern about the adequate representation of African workers was highlighted by an observation attributed to Grobbelaar (1972), who said that about 30 000 Africans had been involved in illegal strikes between 1959 and 1969. The reasons for the increase in the number of illegal strikes are possibly highly complicated. One thing stands out very clearly and it is that this is a very serious indictment of commerce and industry. Here we have the most dramatic expression of a communication problem par excellence.

This essay is an attempt to deal with some aspects of the socio-economic processes of industrialisation and urbanisation as these have affected the African population. This treatment is bound to be sketchy, since particular attention is to be directed at the possible factors which tend to militate against effective communication and to suggest those factors which I consider to promise better organisational hygiene.

Another way of posing the question of the identity of the urban Africans is to ask: Who are the Africans now living in South Africa's urban and industrialised areas? This way of asking the question is for the simple reason that the first question tends to generate more heat than light. Responses to this question have been many and varied. Some observers will tell us that the African is a superstitious simpleton with very little initiative; some will tell us with an air of expertise that his psychology and culture are so different that an elementary course in cultural anthropology would help us out of our partic-ular difficulties; yet others will talk in terms of the 'detrib-alised', the 'transitional' or the 'attention-getting elites'. If we persisted in asking the question, we would probably be reminded that a Motswana carrying an executive briefcase is a Motswana at heart. There are those who would tell us that the urban African is a myth or a monster created by nihilistic anarchists. The truth of the matter is that none of these people knows who we are. Perhaps this is an ideal time to make the point that it is not the white 'experts' who are going to provide the answers to this question. It is, I submit, the black scholars of this country who will first of all ask the right sort of questions with a greater probability of arriving at the best answers.

Attempts directed at understanding the African response to industrialisation and urbanisation may be characterised as having been of two types. There have been simplistic and paternalistic explanations represented in prototype by the contributions of Silberbauer (1968). Not so simplistic but equally naive in conception is the study of the so-called personality of the urban African in South Africa by De Ridder (1961). The second type of contributions has been less ambitious in both design and intention. These contributions will be referred to a little later in this discussion.

A meaningful way of attempting to answer this question appears to be one which recognises its complexity. It seems most useful always to say whether one is attempting a sociological analysis, a cultural-anthropological one, or a social-psychological one, among others, with the added recognition that all these facets are part of a complex existential experience.

The Great Fish River in 1770 and Beyond

South Africa's controversial history tells us that the first recorded encounter between Africans and whites was on the banks of the Great Fish River in 1770. That in many respects tragic and historic event was followed by a history of conflict and disputes whose fallout is still part and parcel of the South African socio-political fabric. After those deeply distressing years came Kimberley and Johannesburg to initiate the denouement of the South African drama.

10

As a part result of that history, Moolman (1971) estimates,[1] by 1970, 55% and 85% (Africans and whites respectively) were living and/or working in the urban areas of South Africa, and 10% of the then African population was in the urban areas by the turn of the present century. What emerges from this last observation is the fact that Africans have been exposed to the influences of urbanisation and industrialisation for well over half a century. Since it is to be expected that these people came into these areas with their own cultural heritage, it becomes relevant to try to understand the extent to which Africans have responded to the existence of other socio-cultural alternatives or what Pauw (1963) describes as the 'triangle of forces' (Western culture, traditional culture and urbanisation). Perhaps it should be pointed out that to ask how Africans have responded to these forces should always be qualified by adding that there has always been compulsory encapsulation of the various racial groups, which has tended to create artificial response patterns.

The question relative to the identity of the urban African is one which is not amenable to full scientific treatment at this stage. It is noteworthy that the first full-scale study of Africans in town is represented by the trilogy *Xhosa in Town*, edited by Mayer.[2] Another important contribution is a volume edited by Holleman *et al.* (1964) with contributions by such leading scholars as Mayer, Glass, Wilson and Biesheuvel. What has emerged from

---

[1] Prof. J.H. Moolman, a reasonably respected researcher, was director of the Africa Institute of South Africa, which was established as a non-profit organisation in 1960 in Pretoria.

[2] Precise publication information for the trilogy is not available. The three titles are *The Black Man's Portion* (Reader, 1961), *Townsmen or Tribesmen* (Mayer, 1961) and *The Second Generation* (Pauw, 1963).

these contributions is a recognition that changes have been and are taking place in urban populations.

For example, it has been frequently pointed out that the African in the urban industrialised cities of South Africa may be grouped into two broad categories, with some variations in between. There are the real 'townsmen' and there are the migrants. If we were to characterise the townsmen briefly, we could say that these are the people who have no important links with the rural areas. Their network of significant personal relationships is to be found in the urban areas. The migrants, on the other hand, consist of those people who are generally rural area-oriented (their networks of personal relationships are rurally based) and are more traditionalist in outlook.

One could take this opportunity to comment on the general limitations of studies of Africans by white South Africans. The first of these limitations is an obvious one. It amounts to the fact that the white experience is so existentially distant from the black experience that white workers have to abstract to a very unhealthy extent in order to move beyond the level of mere description to that of analysis and understanding (interpretation). The second limitation arises out of the fact that the economic motive has generally been very active in the decisions relating to the areas of the black experience which whites have chosen for study. Studies have been considered valuable to the extent that they have offered clues relevant to the possible harnessing of the black labour force for the benefit of industry and commerce. The recurrence of the themes 'African abilities', 'motivation' and 'attitudes' is a very clear index of this preoccupation.

Currently, the majority of Africans live in residential areas known variously as 'locations', 'townships' or 'Bantoedorpe'. These are satellite complexes which are dependent on the white city area for their existence. While many people live in family accommodation settings, there are thousands, about 13 000 for Soweto, according to Hellman (1971), who are on the waiting list for family housing. Another group of Africans are those who lead what Prof. Seftel of the Wits Medical School has described as a 'wifeless existence' – the occupants of closed and total institutions such as the controversial Alexandra hostels. Yet another group of Africans live in the backyards of suburbia. The mental health problems associated with these areas of social disengagement are too well known to require detailed documentation. It should suffice to point out that these problems in their day-to-day manifestations require the most vigilant attention of the employers of African labour.

The adaptational lifestyle which has developed as a result of the black experience in South Africa is something which has not yet been studied in depth and must await a future generation of black scholars. In this essay I limit myself to a few observations which I consider relevant to the problem under discussion. My own experience in both clinical and industrial settings has led to the germination of some tentative ideas and formulations (Manganyi, 1972a). These may be stated as follows: The most predominant feature of all the groups I studied was a form of endemic, chronic sense of insecurity coupled with an ideation characterised by helplessness. Even in clinical practice, as I reported in 1970, this anxiety is the most dramatic expression of the sense of existential insecurity. In the absence of statistics, it may confidently be stated that anxiety states and reactive depression with anxiety features tend to be the most common presenting complaints among African psychiatric patients.

From a mental health point of view, the communities within which Africans have to live are some of the most unhygienic. This is easily appreciated since it has become commonplace to observe that they are characterised by a high morbidity rate, featuring alcoholism and other related forms of overindulgence, crime, a spiralling divorce rate and associated problems in the sphere of parent–child relationships. It is also necessary to point out that in the majority of cases the work situations are just as unhygienic. There are decided indications that most organisations are not geared towards the growth and self-fulfilment of individual employees.

Indeed we find that in the life experience of the African, there is hardly any situation in which his sense of self-esteem is nourished. His wife and children may have been forced by conditions beyond his control to lose the modicum of respect which they may have had for him as an effective, self-steering agent in his psychosocial environment. If we were to formulate his psychic status in a phenomenological way, we could say that his subjective experience is one of feeling emasculated. There are other, more positive sides to this picture, such as the Africans' will to survive (resilience).

At this point in the discussion I would like to make the following submission: Some observers have never tired of pointing out that the African is 'by nature' without initiative, that he has a low aspiration level, that he will always say 'yes' when he should have said 'no', that he is emotional and hedonistic, and that he has the uncanny habits of not keeping time and talking around the point. The stock explanation for this lifestyle is that it is in the nature of Africans, that we just have to understand this and we will have made the great discovery.

It may well be that these traits are to be found in some Africans. Does this in itself suggest that these traits reflect a natural, almost genetic predisposition? Some of us are saying that this is not African nature. That there is no such a thing as

African nature. We are saying that these traits and many others are patterns of adaptation to an unfriendly, always threatening environment. We are saying that the best human potential, given the black existential experience, would in all probability develop similar adjustment manoeuvres. Reality demands that we conceptualise the problem as one essentially involving human nature, one involving a universal tendency to adapt to circumstances, however gruesome.

The first part of this essay has presented a fairly sketchy account of some aspects of the processes of urbanisation and industrialisation as these have affected the African in South Africa. This account was intended as a backdrop for some ideas relating to the African response to these processes as well as the discussion of communication problems per se.

Communication and the South African Scene

I pointed out at the outset that communication in industrial and commercial organisations continues to be a thorny problem. I said at that stage that this is a problem of unusual complexity. But it remains true to say that the maximum exploitation of this country's human and other resources will depend in large measure on how problems in this area are understood and tackled. A general comment on the problems of communication in the South African context cannot be out of place.

In order to understand the communication potential of black–white interaction, it is necessary to reconstruct the prototype of this communicative relational possibility. This relationship is very well known to Africans of all types. Let me reconstruct it as follows: Mr Hlungwani and his wife and children are on a Saturday shopping spree for Christmas. They walk into a large departmental store in Johannesburg. They are all in high spirits. Mr Hlungwani wants to give his wife the gift of his dreams: a very lovely frock which he had always promised to buy her. They approach the white store assistant. Even before Mr Hlungwani can initiate a conversation (relay a message), Mrs du Pont responds by mouthing an obviously rude 'Ja?' Surging with repressed anger and resentment, Mr Hlungwani goes on to explain that he is interested in a particular dress for his wife. Mrs du Pont, in the same contemptuous and indifferent tone, tells Mr Hlungwani to go to that other 'Missus' or 'Madam'.

Here we have the prototype of the master–servant communication complex. Let us look at what has actually happened. Mrs du Pont has not succeeded, strictly speaking, in communicating ideas. She has not succeeded in telling Mr Hlungwani that he is welcome to buy whatever he wishes. He has continued to buy out of necessity or habit, or both. She has in fact communicated an emotion (tonal communication) and Mr Hlungwani should have understood the message to mean that he should walk out of the shop. Most South African communication across the colour line is of this nature.

This kind of communication complex is contrary to the ideal kind of communication complex, namely, one which Van den Berg (1971) exposes in his discussion of the psychotherapy relationship. The essential feature of this communication complex is 'communicative equality'. This means, in effect, that the two people involved in the dialogue should experience and recognise themselves as essentially two 'equal' human beings. Neither of them should be condescending in the relationship. It is only when this condition is satisfied that communicative equivalence can be achieved – talking about the same tree, table or what you will. It is not an overstatement to say that our race relations are not of the kind that promote this kind of communication complex.

After these general remarks about the problem of communication in South Africa, we may now direct our attention to problems specific to industry and commerce. In this part of the essay, some ideas are formulated relating first to the important question of the factors which militate against effective communication with African workers. A second set of ideas is concerned with some approaches which may help reduce unhygienic management strategies in the area of communication. The first set of factors are as follows:

1. The ardent search for simple solutions evidenced by the perpetuation of racial myths. This tendency results in the general development of stereotyped kinds of interpersonal relationships with tonal types of communication and poor communication possibilities.

2. The erstwhile fad of developing separate personnel departments and policies specifically for African labour. In most of these departments African personnel administrators are given token executive status while remaining on the executive fringe of an organisation.

3. The existence of unsatisfactory employee-representation machinery. In cases where such machinery has been created, it is again created as a token and not seriously integrated into the total organisational posture.

4. The existence of an unlimited number of unrewarding, frustrating conditions in the work situation vis-à-vis the worker's psychological and other needs.

5. The absence in many large organisations of well-structured employee-counselling services for employees who must be burdened with problems.

In ending this discussion of factors which are not favourable to effective communication, I would like to single out the question of the status of personnel officers for special comment. It is my impression that some organisations have no clear notions (notions that are clearly spelt out) about the status and function of black personnel officers. It is not uncommon to see an advertisement in the local press mentioning that familiarity with legislation governing the employment of Africans will be an important consideration in qualifying for the job. Granted, this, in the nature of South African society, may be an important consideration. I think that in our unique situation, this kind of employer is likely to have communication difficulties with his personnel officer, let alone his other workers. This is the type of employer who is likely to turn his personnel man into a glorified clerk whose main responsibility is to prepare labour turnover returns and extinguish local fires. Surely, one does not require a university degree in the social sciences to do this sort of thing. I will come back to this issue a little later.

It is not particularly difficult to make a social diagnosis. What is difficult is to suggest remedies and perhaps a prognosis. For our present purposes, a presentation of suggested remedies will suffice. As I see it, the most important requirement is a demand for a dramatic change of attitude away from the prescriptions of the 'African nature' type of explanations to the more valid position that the cultural and genetic heritage of the African does not deprive him of the essential humanity that characterises mankind. To achieve this goal, South African society will have to explode all the racial myths which have been so dear to it. It means, in fact, that commerce and industry will have to disrupt the currently unhappy marriage between the economy and political doctrine. In practical terms it means that there must be a progressive recognition of the essential equality of man, whether separately or otherwise. Once the above observations are given due credit, it comes as no surprise that the double-barrelled personnel approach should be replaced by a unitary one.

It should also mean that the African personnel administrator is well integrated into the management team, that he is well trained and remunerated, and that he enjoys freedom and responsibility in the execution of his skills. He should, as it were, be an effective communication medium. This means that organisational structures should be reorganised.

In the area of employee representation, it seems that in addition to the calls for trade union representation, employee–management committees still remain one viable possibility for ensuring effective communication in the absence of better structures. The introduction of such committees should be very well planned and programmed. There should at least be an induction period for members of the committee. Neglect of considerations of this type often results in tragedies of good intentions.

The dire paucity of community mental health services for blacks is a dramatic indication for the employers of labour to introduce bold initiatives in this area. The creation of full-fledged employee-counselling services would constitute a worthwhile investment, and would certainly improve the mental health of employees and contribute to better communication and productivity.

Let us conclude this essay by stating that the urban African's response to urbanisation and industrialisation is likely to grow more complex and dynamic to the extent that there is no telling what the future has in stock for us.

2 | Black Consciousness

The marriage between the words 'black' and 'consciousness' has in some instances led to panic and consternation in certain sections of the South African public. There have been arguments, debates and naggings. It all happened so quickly that some observers have even suggested that the bogey of *swartgevaar* was suddenly becoming real. After this marriage it even became customary for some people of liberal bent to suggest that black South Africans were now turning racialist. In these observations, there appeared at most times to be an insinuation that black people were becoming the ungrateful people that they are known to be by putting the liberals out of work. This kind of reaction is not entirely unexpected when one considers that South African liberalism can only be a form of narcissism – a form of white self-love. People who love themselves can pity only themselves, hardly anybody else.

What, in fact, these people were saying was that they have been fighting for the black cause for a long time, that it had since become second nature to them to do this pious work. How dare the black people disturb the scheme of things by wanting to do the spadework as well as the dirty work themselves. The extent of South African white fathering was dramatised recently when a black organisation demanded that the word 'blacks' be used instead of the notoriously insulting 'non-Whites' or 'non-Europeans'. What happened at that time was very instructive. We were told in so many ways that we should not behave like a naughty little boy who changes his name without the explicit permission of his father. So many theoretical and semantic difficulties were immediately thrown in our faces. We were told even before the Indian population objected that they would feel insulted by being lumped into the black bag. That effort was a unique demonstration of the white people's expertise in hyperbole.

Leaving the white reaction aside for the moment, we may now turn our attention to the actual marriage that took place between the words 'black', 'consciousness' and 'solidarity'. Since it has been suggested that these words might mean damnation or racialism or *swartgevaar*, it becomes necessary to inquire into some of their meanings as understood by us. I should not be misunderstood to be saying that all black people will agree with my understanding of these concepts. It seems to me that the white people have to wait for us to tell them what we mean by these terms just as they have to accept our interpretation of the concepts of African personality and Négritude. When words or concepts become public property they tend to become either clichés or slogans. It is then necessary to remain strictly within the accepted meanings or definitions for purposes of communication. The word which requires definition is 'consciousness'.

According to the *Shorter Oxford English Dictionary*, the following meanings of the word 'consciousness' are given: 'mutual knowledge'; 'knowledge as to which one has the testimony within oneself'; and 'the totality of the impressions, thoughts, and feelings, which make up a person's conscious being'. The first usage, though rare, is of the utmost importance.

In our definition of Black Consciousness there is an implicit recognition of mutual knowledge. This recognition leads us further to that of black solidarity. From mutual knowledge to solidarity is a very short and logical step. But now the question may be asked: mutual knowledge about what? This also is crucial. Before answering this question, it should be stated that Black Consciousness is something about which each black person has evidence (testimony) within himself. This will be developed later. The question about mutual knowledge may now be answered: Black Consciousness should be understood to mean that there is mutuality of knowledge with respect to the 'totality' of impressions, thoughts and feelings of all black people.

Some observations made by some people may create the spurious impression that Black Consciousness primarily refers to awareness of skin colour. This is not a judicious interpretation. My own interpretation is that skin colour in itself and of itself is insignificant. What is important is what the skin actually signifies in sociological and psychological terms. The skin only becomes significant in these terms as body. There can be no bickering about the existential significance of the body. It is precisely for this reason that Black Consciousness has no choice but to start from the existential fact of the black body.

This is a recognition of the fact that it is the sociological schema of the black body which has in so many ways determined part of our experience of being-in-the-world. In other words, it has determined part of the totality of the experience of which we are being called upon to be conscious. In terms of the body, then, we may say that we are being called upon to experience our black bodies in a revitalised way. We are being called upon to change the negative sociological schema imposed upon us by whites.

I have often said that the existential fact of the black body has also meant certain specific ways of relating to the world and to others. This relating may be understood as involving both positive and negative features. In its negative form we recognise the fact of a specific form of suffering – that of having been a colonised people. It stands to reason that part of our consciousness of being black people amounts to a mutual knowledge of this suffering at the hands of white domination. We must hasten to say that this consciousness of mutual suffering must not be mistaken for self-pity, for that would be a tragedy. The black people share the experience of having been abused and exploited. This is part of our consciousness.

Consciousness of our experience of suffering also means on the positive side that we share the mutual knowledge of wanting to escape from this suffering. To the extent that we are conscious of being black people will we be more in a position to improve on our lot. At this stage, one would like to point out that Black Consciousness is time-bound. This means that it is characterised by its temporality. It is, as it were, consciousness of past, present and future. The fact of the temporality of Black Consciousness is very important, and is accounted for by the following observations: If we should only talk in terms of the mutual knowledge of the fact of suffering (both past and present), we could be accused of oversimplifying. What emerges on reflection is that the consciousness of being black must also include the fact of our contribution to culture, for I am loath to talk in terms of civilisation. For us then, Black Consciousness in its temporality includes the consciousness of our cultural heritage. It has been said often enough that African cultures were assaulted almost beyond recognition. It has not been said often enough that Black Consciousness must also include as part of its recognition of suffering this fact.

If Black Consciousness simply amounted to a mere recognition of this historicity, it would be nothing more than ancestor worship. We said that it has its temporal dimensions of past, present and future. It follows that for Black Consciousness to be an 'active presence' in the world, it has to deal with the present and the future. What may be said about Black Consciousness and the present? Inter alia, it may be said that in its expression of the present it is first of all mutual knowledge about its historicity. Second, it amounts to a recognition and the desire to re-establish community feeling. This is generally what is meant by the word 'solidarity'. Some people feel themselves very threatened by this development. It should not constitute a threat of any kind, because it is a logical result of a common existential experience. Where there is mutual knowledge it should come as no surprise if there should be solidarity. A negative way of looking at this development is to say that this solidarity is only against white people. People who subscribe to this view fail to go on to say that this is only a historical necessity. It immediately becomes clear that we are not in any way to blame for this fact. Theoretically, Black Consciousness and solidarity could have been neutral. This, however, is hardly possible since in large measure Black Consciousness and solidarity must be considered a response to white consciousness and solidarity (racialism).

Black Consciousness and solidarity must be seen by us as phenomena that are positive in themselves. This means that they are desirable even outside considerations involving white domination and racialism. References to these developments as 'racialism' become meaningless in the face of this recognition. Nobody should ever have had any right to tell anybody else that he should not be aware of himself as being. Black Consciousness and solidarity as expressed in the present should also mean something in addition. They should mean continuity with the past and the future. Something has been said about the past already; it is now necessary to make a few remarks on the future.

Our orientation with respect to the future is of the utmost importance. It is a commonplace to say that what will happen in the future will be determined in large measure by what Black Consciousness and solidarity mean to us today. At the time of writing, it is possible to spell out a few thoughts on this matter. An idea which appeals to my fancy amounts to saying that Black Consciousness and solidarity must mean to us that we have to re-examine the forms assumed by personal and community relationships in our midst. This is necessary for the simple reason that we have the mutual knowledge about the assault on the sense of community that befell us. Our spirit of communalism was gradually eroded until we were left with individualism and its stablemate materialism. Solidarity among other things means that we as a people have to share. This sharing is all-embracing, since it involves the sharing not only of material things but also of suffering and the possible joys of being-black-in-the-world. It may now be said that in the past we have not shared as we should have because in order to share, it is imperative to have the mutuality of knowledge of suffering which is now anchored in Black Consciousness.

There are many important considerations which go against the notion of the significance of tribal groupings. In this age of power politics and major powers, the grouping of people into tribes must be seen as something which amounts to a crude experiment. The money economics of the present century definitely provide the most convincing evidence against such experiments. We as black people have our own evidence, which should tell us that tribalism is dead because this is the twentieth century. No efforts on a grand scale to reintroduce tribalism will succeed in the long run. What kind of evidence do we have? The primary evidence revolves around the fact of mutual knowledge which is now expressing itself as Black Consciousness and solidarity. We do know that there are people who have gone to great lengths to demonstrate that the various tribal groupings in South Africa are culturally and linguistically very different. This has been used as the major premise for current South African policies. We were not asked whether we did accept that this is a matter of unusual significance to us. There is sufficient respectable evidence to support the idea that there is a great deal that is common to all African cultures on the African continent let alone in South Africa. One such a common denomination is African ontology, discussed elsewhere in this collection. Other uniformities arise from the unique type of suffering which has been part of our common experience on the African continent.

We have to be unified by our common desire to take the initiative in deciding and determining our future and that of future generations of black South Africans. We have mutual knowledge of the ways in which we have been deprived of this right. In their temporal dimensions, Black Consciousness and solidarity must mean something more than sheer nostalgia. In their present and future thrusts, they must mean the birth of a new creativity. It needs no gainsaying to point out that this must be a broadly based type of creativity covering all the significant sectors of our existence. The implications of this last statement for black people are many. Black Consciousness and solidarity must be understood as expressive of a new kind of responsibility. This responsibility covers all the important areas of our socio-political existence. We also have to get away from the political scapegoating which has characterised our existence for the past decade. What this means in practice is that we should not be saying that the white man has closed all the avenues for political expression. When we say this we should normally go on to say that this recognition does not mean that we should recognise our communities as simply dead. Life is not only political. Possibilities for self-improvement as a people should have been explored before we simply threw in the towel.

There are two important issues which should be raised relating to Black Consciousness and solidarity. The first is the relationship between consciousness and action. This relationship is often neglected by exponents of Black Consciousness. The neglect of this aspect almost amounts to a lack of a clear formulation of the actual practical meaning of solidarity. In addition to the relationship between mutual knowledge and solidarity there exists the connotation of action in solidarity. In other words, one has to be thinking of a consciousness which leads to action. It is not a primary consideration for us to point out the forms which should be assumed by the action involved in black solidarity. We are content to make the observation that such action as may be expressive of this solidarity will require all the ingenuity and creativity of we as a people are capable.

The reader may feel obliged to ask whether in the nature of our actual circumstances it is at all possible to indulge in creative action. Admittedly, the problems raised by this question are complex but significant. What this question amounts to is to reveal the possible significance of the problem of freedom vis-à-vis Black Consciousness and solidarity. This is the second issue which I said I intended to raise. The problem of freedom may not be discussed without reference to its overall significance in human affairs. This is our next task.

Human freedom is a pet subject of existential philosophy, however defined. This problem has also found its way into phenomenologically and existentially oriented psychothera-pies. For example, we find it being a major concern of Sartre's in *Being and Nothingness* (1956), Frankl's in *Psychotherapy and Existentialism* (1967), May's in *Psychology and the Human Dilemma* (1967), Merleau-Ponty's in *Phenomenology of Perception* (1962) and Fromm's in *Escape from Freedom* (1941). Besides these academic contributions and many others, the problem must always be considered one which is of interest to the lay public. Since this is a subject of such public significance, I intend to spend a little more time discussing it. We will limit our discussion to some of the ideas of Frankl since these appear to be the most relevant for the topic under discussion. In this book and others, Frankl makes a number of observations concerning freedom. The most important observation on freedom is contained in the following statement:

> Needless to say, the freedom of a finite being such as man is a freedom within limits. Man is not free from conditions, be they biological or psychological or sociological in nature. But he is, and always remains, free to take a stand toward these conditions; he always retains the freedom to choose his attitude toward them. Man is free to rise above the plane of somatic and psychic determinants of his existence. (Frankl, 1967: 3)

Frankl is talking about the ultimate freedom expressed generally in what he describes as 'attitudinal values'. His main contention is that a human being has potential to transcend his existen-tial limitations to his freedom by taking a stand (free choice) vis-à-vis these limitations. The question now arises whether this assertion may be considered one which is generally valid in any situation where there are such limitations.

To us, it seems that Frankl may in a sense be accused of having indulged in an interesting and profound abstraction. Although this abstraction appears to have been stated with conviction, it seems to us to remain an open question which calls for more reflection. As he pointed out, limitations to freedom may arise at a number of levels. These limitations may be somatic (bodily), they may be psychic or they may be sociological. One should in all fairness hasten to add that limitations in one of these dimensions must always have far-reaching effects on the possibilities of freedom in the other two dimensions. It would appear that it is relatively easier for one to take a stand (develop an attitude) towards somatic and psychic limitations since these tend to raise higher-order type of questions. This is understand-able, since such questions as are raised will tend to focus on the obscurities of the meaning of life. Here again, not all human beings are capable of asking these questions, least of all taking a stand against an unalterable fate.

Sociological limitations to freedom are more instructive. An example may well illustrate this point. A healthy slave would be sold to a slave owner. That act would signify for the slave the beginning of excruciating limitations on his freedom. Taking a stand in the face of these limitations immediately implies the existence of several possible choices, for one may not be said to be taking a stand when there is no alternative course of action. A further qualification appears necessary: The available alternatives should include a number of positive possible attitudinal stands. These alternatives may only be positive and meaningful to the extent that they will improve the lot of the slave – redeem part of his existential freedom. Theoretically, it should be possible for the slave to adopt the attitude that he is going to fight his master in order to regain his freedom. The slave recognises the futility of such a stand

and may well slide into despair and indifference. This despair and indifference may express themselves in various forms of hedonism, which may never be considered an expression of freedom. Could one say that one is expressing one's ability to transcend limitations on one's freedom when one despairs and becomes indifferent? A positive stand should be supported by rational and affective conviction. This condition is not met in the case of despair and indifference.

The point may be made that it is possible for certain resourceful individuals to take a stand against what for all intents and purposes may be provisional limitations to their freedom. A patient who knows that he is going to die within a few days may well brace himself up – may take a stand because death in its obscurity may come to present an absurd kind of freedom. The situation is different for a slave who has the knowledge that his parents were slaves, that he is a slave and his children are going to be slaves. The time perspective here is so different that there appear to be only two alternatives. The first, which is not always possible, is to wish to lose everything by being prepared for a physical death – committing suicide or taking up arms against his master. The second is the more usual process of committing suicide in small doses represented so often in hedonism.

It therefore appears that it is not useful to take a stand as long as such an attitude does not result in conscious action because that becomes indifference. What are the implications of our discussion of freedom with respect to Black Consciousness and solidarity? We have a duty to be conscious of our responsibility to deal with limitations to our freedom. Black Consciousness and solidarity must mean a posture which will express a movement away from indifference and despair to rational, organised activity. Frankl has suggested in addition to his position on freedom that there are other values in life which may be realised. He suggests as one of these what he describes as 'creative' values – what we give to the world. I suggested that this in its broadest sense must be considered as one of the possibilities of the awareness of being black. Another possibility away from indifference is an increased sensitivity to one's surroundings ('experiential values'). The creative potential of black South Africans will be measured against their action potential.

I would like to comment on one issue which has generated more heat than light. Some people, even black people, have wondered whether a separatist posture is essential to Black Consciousness and solidarity. It should be obvious to anybody that black people and white people will continue to live together as long as there is life on this planet. A separatist posture should never be understood to negate the existence of other racial groups. This posture would seem to arise from the fact that we as a people want to indulge unhindered in self-reflection and in self-definition, and we are putting conditions on how this should take place. The essential condition is that only people who share our mutual knowledge should actively participate in these activities. This position is capable of being abused by both white and black people. Nobody should consider this to be a very important fact, since it is only a side issue.

In sum, we may say that the mutual knowledge which is Black Consciousness and solidarity is not by design racialism. It is a way of relating, of being-black-in-the-world in its temporality of past, present and future.

3 | Us and Them

Before the advent of the policy of separate development, some observers believed South Africa to be a multiracial national state. The historic victory of the Nationalist Party in 1948 changed all that. It is now common in certain circles in South Africa to talk in terms of multinationalism. It is claimed by some exponents of the policy of separate development that South Africa is a country consisting of many races, ethnic groups, languages and cultures. This, in fact, is true. The exponents go on to suggest that it is in recognition of this diversity that South Africa must be Balkanised into several national (ethnic) units.

Policy affecting the country as a whole may be decided on the basis of the above categories. It is questionable whether individual relations and group relationships between blacks and whites are motivated and supported by such considerations. These relationships appear to be determined at much lower and simpler levels. This seems to arise from the fact that in race-conscious environments, such as ours, it is difficult for individuals and groups to develop ways of action, feeling and thinking which transcend the categorical relationships involved in us (in-group) and them (out-group). 'Us' and 'them' consti-tute, in our society, a linguistic attitudinal form, expressive of

distance and relation, and as such may be considered to be in the
domain of Buber's philosophy of dialogue.

It will be shown in this essay that these categorical relations
are related, in our society, to different experiences – two modes
of being-in the world. These two existential experiences
may be characterised as being-black-in-the-world and
being-white-in-the-world. It has to be admitted that the primary
mode of being-in-the-world, of existing, is a given, and is therefore universal. The differences between the white and black
experiences of being-in-the-world have arisen because of the
fact that man, unlike other lower animals, is a historical being.

There will be time to return to the above issues. But before
that is undertaken, I would like to make some more general
observations about the South African social environment.

The general issues relating to man's tribalism have been
adequately treated by Niebuhr (1966). The concerns here are
more specific than his, and relate to a particular environment
with its historical and cultural contingencies.

At this stage, there is an important question which requires
the most dispassionate kind of reflection, and which may be
formulated as follows: What is the most distinctive feature of
the South African environment? The answer is to be found not
in the public statements of politicians but in the formulations
of the psychology of ideological totalism as described by Lifton
(1961: 418), who has commented as follows:

> Any ideology – that is, any set of emotionally-charged
> convictions about man and his relationship to the natural
> and supernatural world – may be carried by its adherents
> in a totalistic direction. But this is most likely to occur with
> those ideologies which are most sweeping in their content
> and most ambitious – or messianic – in their claims.

Several criteria (psychological themes) may be used to judge the extent of ideological totalism in an environment. Briefly, these may be presented as follows.

Most important is the criterion relating to the extent of *milieu control*. This may take various forms, such as are represented in censorship (communication) and indoctrination-cum-education. A totalistic environment tends to develop a *mystical imperative*. This mystique, generally considered to represent a more all-inclusive and higher purpose, may be God and/or Western civilisation. A criterion related to mystical manipulation in totalist environments is the *demand for purity*. This requirement results in a two-valued orientation, pure party-men as against communists and agitators – a pure race in contrast to an impure one. The demand for purity also leads to the demand for the *total exposure* of individuals in the community. This demand for exposure is related to the claim of totalistic environments to complete ownership of individuals (their minds) in that milieu.

The other criteria may be stated briefly as follows: There is the active attempt to create an *aura of sacredness* around an ideology and its basic assumptions. This is achieved by active prohibition of serious questioning of the ideology and its assumptions. Associated with ideologically totalist environments is a marked tendency to *load the language* with a limited number of emotionally overloaded clichés. Overloading of the language may manifest itself in phrases and words such as 'the maintenance of law and order' and 'agitators' and 'communists'. A most dramatic characteristic of ideological totalism is the *elevation of doctrine* over the individual. This is evidenced by a sustained encroachment on individual liberties. A totalistic environment *maintains a distinction* between 'the people' (whose rights and existence are recognised) and the 'non-people' (whose existence and rights are not seriously considered).

That South Africa is a totalist country has been said often enough. What has not been said is that there are important issues raised by that recognition. It has not been said often and loud enough that the ideological totalism of apartheid is radically more total in its control of the lives of black South Africans. The ideological totalism of apartheid expresses itself differentially in the white and black sectors of South African society. By design? It has not been said that below the superficial and obvious crudeness of the practical application of separate development there lies a very sophisticated and subtle tiger: psychic manipulation. There are two real dangers, among others, in this form of psychic manipulation. The first danger relates to the fact that a totalistic environment tends to lower the integrative status of a community. This means that such environments become less and less supportive of the individuals that live in them. Integration is rapidly replaced by chaos, by a high morbidity rate and by increasing failures by individuals to constitute meaningful lived-space. The second danger is that there can be no doubt that the overall effects of chronic and subtle psychic manipulation must have a decisive impact on the general vitality and psychic health of future generations of South Africans. This observation in itself is not alarming. What gives the observation its nightmarish quality is the further thought that it may well take a 'second coming' to undo the harm.

The issue as to whether South Africa qualifies for inclusion among ideologically totalist environments is not to be under-stood as constituting an academic polemic. It is raised here because it is possibly the most important attribute of South African society which must be taken into account in any attempt at understanding the us and them categories as well as the forms taken by the black experience of being-black-in-the-world.

Being-in-the-World in Its Historicity

In order to reflect on the development of the us and them categories (these being categories of interaction, of interpersonal relationships) it is essential to deal with the historically available modes of being-in-the-world. It was pointed out earlier that being-in-the-world (existence) is a given. This means in effect that the basic structure of existence is historical. It is specifically man's historicity and his being a decisive being (man decides what to become) which have infused variations on this given existential structure. It is these two factors which have made it possible, if not imperative, for us to say that there is a mode of existence (of being-in-the-world) which may be characterised as being-white-in-the-world and being-black-in-the-world. There is sufficient documentation of the fact that the history of being-in-the-world (*in-der-Welt-sein*) of the black and white races of the world is different. This history has been so different, in fact, that one is justified to talk in terms of a black and white existential experience. These observations are to be substantiated at a later stage.

Dialogue and Relation

Existence (*dasein*) is dialogue: relation. This means that an individual is always transacting with his environment. In phenomenological reflection this idea is not novel. It is central. In order to understand this idea more fully, it is necessary to bring it down to the level of individual existence. The individual, if he should be healthy, is a dialogue: He is always relating. Van den Berg (1964) has vividly conveyed this fact in his description of the psychiatric patient. He, among others, has helped us identify the major aspects which constitute the structure of existences, of lived-space. Another way of making this point is to say that dialogue (relation) may be established at four different levels. An individual has to relate himself first to his body as existential fact. In addition to this dialogue with his body, relations have to be established with fellowmen and sometimes God (god), with objects (material culture) and with time. A brief consideration of these constituents of the existential structure follows.

The Body

In order to understand the nature of the differences between the black and white experiences, it is necessary to deal with their respective experiences in relation to the body. Little recognition has been given to the social-psychology of the body outside attempts to describe difficulties and privileges associated with skin colour. This trend is unpardonable, in view of the fact that an extensive treatment of this subject is currently available. (See, for example, Fisher and Cleveland [1968b]. Another respectable treatment of this subject is available in Merleau-Ponty [1962]. Shontz [1969] raises some pertinent theoretical and empirical questions relating to this problem.) I have dealt with the body image elsewhere (Manganyi, 1972a). Here I hope to pay particular attention to the social-psychology of the body or, more aptly, the sociological schema described in the Introduction. (Kouwer [1953] refers to this schema.)

One of the legacies of colonialism in Africa has been the development of the dichotomy relating to the body, namely, the 'bad' and the 'good' body. The white man's body has been projected as the 'good' – the standard, the norm of beauty and of accomplishment. Not only the body proper, but its periphery; its embellishments have also been recognised as such. On the contrary, the black body has always been projected as the 'bad', as being inferior and unwholesome.

The implications of this dichotomy are many and varied. An important result of this state of affairs was the development of two different sociological schemas of the body: One of these schemas was black and bad and the other was white and good. This distinction has for a long time affected the texture of interpersonal relationships across the colour line. It is understandable why the black body generally acted as a *barrier* to effective communication while the white body thrived on its *appeal* characteristics. Although the body is distinctly ambiguous in its essential nature, rigid and categorical characterisation in the contact situation has resulted in the limitation for *individualisation* of the black body. Under ideal conditions of the good body, the body becomes for the individual a point of view (Merleau-Ponty, 1962). This means that the individual schema predominates over the sociological schema. This last condition is one which has obtained in white societies for a long time. In black communities, on the other hand, through the artificial and unnatural predominance of the sociological schema the individual schema has become traumatised and ceases to be a point of view, of telling the world who one is.

A desirable balance between the individual and socio-logical schemas of the body is mandatory for psychic balance, competence and positive self-steering behaviour. Since the body constitutes the existential nexus of personal existence, it comes as no surprise that the black body, with its essentially negative prescribed attributes, has not always generated competence. Thus it is that the self-fulfilling prophecy of the white man – that he is competent and superior while the African is 'by nature' inferior and incompetent – tends to take on the semblance of a reality. This conclusion is expressed as follows by Schlemmer (1971: 162): '. . . lifelong experience of subservience, the daily struggle for existence, the massive proportions of white power and the superior morale of whites, have produced divisions and conflicts within black communities, and a general feeling of disspiritedness [*sic*] and helplessness, all of which are functional for the continuation of white supremacy'.

There are people who have discredited the 'Black is Beautiful' campaign. Since this reaction is a result of ignorance, ignorance about the significance of the sociological schema of the body, it is perhaps pardonable. We as blacks must now say with all the conviction at our command that a massive and creative campaign is essential to alter the negative sociological schema of the black body. This is not only desirable from the point of view of its inherent aesthetic potential, but also because of the unlimited social-psychological significance of the body as existential fact-situation.

It may now be pointed out that the body, in the contact between whites and blacks, has always provided a splendid medium for the development of the us and them categories. The body has always determined distance and relation (dialogue). Through the sociological schemas, it has always acted on its barrier or appeal characteristics. Distancing and relating.

Without going into details, one last point should be made with respect to the body. A negative sociological schema, and by the same token a negative individual schema, inevitably leads to an unhealthy objectification of the body. This means that the individual begins to experience his body as an object. He experiences his body as though it were something outside himself. This is an expected result of the predominance of the sociological schema over the individual schema. A healthy individual rarely experiences his body as an object, as something outside himself. It is only in pathological states (illness) that the body is experienced as alien. During acute illness the body is objectified to an unusual extent.

As long as the two sociological schemas of the body exist side by side, as is likely to happen for a long time in South Africa, it will remain true to say that the body will continue to foster and nourish the us and them categories. This means that there will continue to be being-black-in-the-world and being-white-in-the-world. Two existential experiences.

Of more immediate significance, however, are considerations concerning the black body. Nobody should accuse us of suggesting that the black body is superior to any other biological type. All we wish to say is that the negative prescribed sociological schema (with its barrier attributes) must be replaced by a more realistic sociological schema (with appeal attributes) defined and developed by black people.

The Individual in Society

Every individual in society is related to his fellowmen at a number of entry points: family, neighbourhood and ideally the whole of the community of which he is a member. It has been shown that these primary and secondary forms of relationship are culture-bound. In Africa, there has been sufficient documentation of the characteristic primary group structures such as the extended family and kinship systems, as well as the secondary group processes involved in communalism (corporate personality). At the level of the relationship between the individual and his fellowmen, we recognise a polarity of approaches. The white approach is characterised by the primacy of the individual (individualism), while the black approach was characterised by the primacy of the community.

The conquest of blacks in South Africa and the subsequent socio-political history has resulted, inter alia, in the destruction of African traditional approaches in this area. The main point I wish to raise in this respect is that outside the very real problems associated with money economies, the political suppression of blacks has had one overriding result, which may be summarised as follows.

The effective control of black political initiatives since the early sixties has meant that blacks relinquish any community-oriented objectives. This destruction of community feeling was achieved by means of a number of well-studied strategies. One of these has been the stifling of effective and articulate popular leadership. What became of this effort, as I hope to show later, was an individualism more malignant than that found within white elitist capitalist societies.

The rise of the individualistic and materialistic ethic is something which is essentially alien to being-black-in-the-world. The call for Black Consciousness and solidarity must be considered a medium for the creative development of individual and community dignity. Black Consciousness and solidarity will be meaningful only to the extent that they ensure the effective return of the individual to the community. That is where he belongs. In terms of the existential structure suggested here, being-black-in-the-world means, inter alia, that we must change our modes of relating to our black bodies and communities from those prescribed by the dominant culture. It obviously must remain a matter of profound indifference to us whether these changes are acceptable to the dominant culture.

Being-in-the-World with Objects

It was pointed out that existence is dialogue-relation. It has been shown that this relation-dialogue (being-in-the-world) has been and is different for blacks and whites. This has been shown to be the case with respect to the body as well as the larger community. There is another existential category which may be studied in order to demonstrate the difference in modes of being-in-the-world – the category of being-in-the-world with objects or things. The issues raised with respect to man and objects are closely related to those that were made concerning individualism. A well-known stablemate of individualism is materialism. Now, it seems to me to be a simple matter to recognise that attitudes towards objects (also, material culture) are fundamentally determined by the general cultural ethos of a community, namely, whether it be individualistic, capitalistic or communalistic.

The noted distortion of the relationship between the individual and his community also meant a dramatic change in his system of values. Under ideal conditions, man's relationship with an object may generally be said to be decided by the object's aesthetic and utility value. This principle is violated whenever individuals are deprived of dignity and self-respect, and are, for some reason or other, unable to activate the spiritual core (not necessarily religious) of their selfhood. Whenever this noetic dimension is allowed to lie dormant or is not activated,[1] a veritable distortion of the being-in-the-world with objects relationship arises. Such a distortion may easily be shown to arise whenever individuals find themselves in situations where the more intangible values are relegated to an inferior status. These individuals have been shown to develop a tendency to validate themselves in terms of external, easily identifiable criteria. It becomes obvious on close study of such people that their values system did not arise at any stage from

[1] Noesis is a notion in metaphysical philosophy that means 'understanding' or 'intellect'.

the activating core of the noetic dimension but is a direct result of naked sociological considerations entirely beyond their control.

In the socially pathological situations of the kind described here, it is not uncommon to find that a poet is considered a lesser being than the Mercedes Benz-driving business tycoon. This universal tragedy is perhaps without comparison in its magnitude as manifested in South Africa's black communities. The psychological impact of the white dominant culture on the relation between blacks and objects may be formulated in the following way: The white culture has over a number of centuries proclaimed the superiority of its cultural heritage. This attitude gave birth to some of the most unfortunate 'hang-ups' experienced by blacks the world over. One of the results was that success, being a white prerogative, also became white by definition. A white norm. For the successful black man, the relationship between him and objects (material culture) moved from the purely aesthetic-utilitarian level to the distinctly pathological-compensatory level. In this process an inversion took place. Instead of the given existential relationship between man and objects in which man continues to decide on the nature of the dialogue, this time it is as though the objects were doing the deciding, assisted, of course, by the white dominant culture.

The development of a favourable man–object relationship will require a regeneration of community feeling – the active promotion of creative, experiential and attitudinal values which are not consonant with individualism and materialism. This objective may not be realised within the current existential structures created by the white dominant culture. It seems logical for black people to adopt a posture of positive, creative 'isolation'. Group introspective analysis – an inward look – is mandatory for us in any attempt at restructuring our values system (as effectively described by Khoapa [1972]).

Being-in-the-World-in-Time

A brief comment on the existential category of time is now appropriate. The existential character of time may be formulated as follows: Time is real only in terms of its primeval relationship with space. In this combination, time and space constitute an individual's lived-space (existence). Ideally, an individual should be free to constitute his lived-space on the basis of the open appeal of time. An individual has potential. Time appeals to this potential to be realised freely. Such potential may only be realised in freedom-in-security (a dialectic).

Once the condition of freedom-in-security is not met, a disturbance of the relationship between man and time is introduced. Without going into details, it may be said that this condition has not been met in the black experience for more than three centuries. There has not been freedom-in-security in our relationship with time, in the ways in which we have been 'allowed' to constitute our lived-space, in our response to the open appeal of time to actualise our potential as people. In the absence of freedom-in-security, planning becomes existentially meaningless and the individual life becomes provisional. When this happens, people live as though they were immortal, as though death were a fiction. Other disturbances associated with this distortion of the man–time relationship are those relating to initiative and achievement. In this respect, it is to be noted that individual initiative as well as the desire for achievement become accidental rather than purely volitional acts.

The black and white modes of being-in-the-world-in-time have been and are different. The white dominant cultures have enshrined freedom-in-security for members of their kind while ensuring the maximum absence of this condition for blacks. Thus it is that the primeval relationship between man and time is disturbed in the black existential experience. This is indeed a very serious matter requiring the most serious reflection and action on our part.

Us and Them

'Us' and 'them' remain basic categories of socio-political inter-action here and elsewhere. They are categories of distance and relation. The distance between blacks and whites is real. There is a black mode of being-in-the-world. The relation between blacks and whites, though inescapable, is of a categorical nature; it is in the nature of stereotyping ('us' and 'them'). Since these conclusions are true, dialogue between these two groups will remain super-ficial for a long time. This is understandable because there will always be two frames of reference (two existential experiences) with regard to any important issue which arises. To take a topical issue, there will be no immediate agreement between blacks and whites regarding the calls for Black Consciousness and soli-darity. White South Africans interpret this as racialism, while we regard the same phenomena as a medium for positive, creative and defensive racialism which is opposed to the traditional nega-tive racialism practised by whites.

In our attempt to regain our lost dignity as a people, there are four fundamental levels at which an attack must be launched: There is an urgent need for serious reflection on how best we can redirect our age-old attitudes in respect of our black beautiful bodies, our community responsibilities, our attitudes towards the material culture and our relationship with time.

4 | Being-Black-in-the-World

The question regarding the usefulness and psychological meaningfulness of the concept of African personality remains essentially undecided. A recent review of its status by a noted scholar, though probably the most well formulated in the literature, poses more questions than are answered: LeVine (1970), whose guarded reserve is evident, has lucidly isolated some of the most thorny issues attendant on the concept and its development.

Areas of specific agreement between this author and myself are the following: First, all reasonable and informed observers will agree that part of the stalemate in the development of the concept may in large measure be attributed to partisan stereo-typing such as is represented in the contributions of Carothers (1953) and the Johannesburg psychologist, J.C. de Ridder (1961). Second, with respect to personality structure, LeVine makes the important observation that there are various possible levels of abstraction in the analysis and description of personality which must always be recognised in any attempt at formulating personality characteristics of a group of people. This valid point is not always recognised. Third, I also support the proposition that African societies and cultures as compared to others outside Africa are in important respects distinctive.

The methodological problems attendant on the concept of African personality in its psychological connotations are very aptly expressed by LeVine (1970) in the following statement:

> Thus 'the African personality' cannot be more than a matter of statistical tendency and is likely to show less uniformity across African populations than do patterns of culture.

Contributions in the area have tended to highlight an obtrusive conceptual mix-up between 'patterns of culture' and what some authors have described as 'personality'. This mix-up has been a direct result of the failure to conceptualise personality structure as being essentially stratified, as being made of core and outer possible levels of abstraction.

The apparent and real semantic and other problems associated with the concept of African personality appear upon reflection to be of a fairly simple nature. These difficulties vanish from the scene the moment due recognition is given to the following considerations: Rather than ask the unwieldy question: Is there an African personality? it appears more legitimate to reformulate this as: Is there an experiential repertoire which may be considered distinctly African? I will return to this question a little later.

As another observation it may be stated that the concept of African personality as defined by white observers is foreign to us as Africans. As defined and understood by leading Africans the concept refers more inclusively to a lifestyle. In our view, African personality should be nothing more or less than what

Senghor (1966) has popularised as Négritude. His definition of Négritude makes the identity of the African personality unmistakably clear:

> It is – as you can guess from what precedes – the sum of the cultural values of the black world; that is, a certain active presence in the world, or better, in the universe. It is, as John Reed and Clive Wake call it, a certain 'way of relating oneself to the world and to others'. (Senghor, 1966)

It should be readily admitted that in this, the only legitimate interpretation of the concept, there is no cause or reason for any misunderstanding. Confusion has arisen because the De Ridders (1961) have attempted and preferred to see in this concept strictly psychological properties. It appears to have escaped the notice of the De Ridders that it may probably make sense to study the personality of an individual but hardly that of a million people. It should be clear that statistical central tendencies do not tell us much about Africans, let alone their personality!

Since it may not be easy to settle so emotionally charged an issue as the one under discussion, it may be necessary to supply more supportive arguments. Those who may be interested in the behavioural manifestations of Négritude could better conceptualise their area of interest as one which primarily involves adaptational lifestyles. Such a shift would ensure the realisation of a number of objectives, one of which would be a recognition of the fact that Africans are part of the human race, and that contrary to popular notions there is a trend more towards genetic convergence at this stage in the history of man than towards divergence (Tobias, 1972).

This last point would not require documentation if we did not have to contend with almost universal racial bigotry in the guise of respectable scientific knowledge. A second objective appears to be a rather unfortunate one, since it is not always cordial to remind people that they colonised one. Detractors will tell us that this question of having been colonised is a historical platitude, that in fact nobody was or is to blame. It remains fundamentally true to insist on a fresh recognition of the historical fact of colonialism since this historical exigency may make certain currently less understood realities about being-black-in-the-world understandable.

An approach of the kind suggested here would appear to promise a greater probability of meaningfully studying the African mode of relating, the African mode of being-in-the-world, the African mode of relating (dialogue) to the body, to others, to objects and to space and time. There cannot be any doubt that being-in-the-world with a black body has transformed the essential forms of the relationships among the different existential categories such as time and objects. The problem as I see it involves the ontological study of black existence. Before such a radical statement is made, the following further points should be made.

The Active Presence that Is Négritude

We accept Senghor's (1966) contention that Négritude is 'the sum of the cultural values of the black world' and that this totality of cultural values is a 'certain active presence' in the world. Unlike most white observers, we consider this presence to be a positive one to the extent that Senghor could go on to describe Négritude as a 'humanism' of the twentieth century. Some observations concerning the ontological significance of culture will not be inappropriate.

Ontologically, culture may be understood as constituting the most concrete medium for the structuring of the dialogue between man and the universe. This recognition of culture as the primary medium for the constituting of man–world relations leads one to the conclusion that since there are many cultural patterns in the world, it should come as no matter for controversy to say that there are variations in the mode of being-in-the-world. This notion is not as radical as it appears at first sight, since it has been convincingly suggested that there is a feminine mode of being-in-the-world. Some sceptics may invoke biology in an attempt to take the wind out of my sails. This kind of scapegoating will not prove to be novel.

That questions of biology, of heredity, of biological determinism, of the superiority and inferiority of one biological group (race) as against others still constitute matters for time-consuming debate has been highlighted by the so-called Jensen controversy so ably presented by Tobias (1972) recently. We brush aside with gusto the puerile suggestions of the Jensens of this world who would let us believe that biological determinism is the main existential category accounting for differences in modes of being-in-the-world. Radical reflection on the contrary tells us that the issue is much more complex. Very little attention should be paid to these detractors. What is urgently required is to establish whether there is a distinctly black mode of existing – whether one may identify an ontological structure that may be associated with being-black-in-the-world.

There are of course academics and laypeople who will, because of some unshakeable racialistic convictions, be prepared for an outright inquisition before admitting the possible existence of a strictly African ontology. This reaction is to be treated with contempt since it will come as no surprise to us. Our experience has taught us that these are likely to

50

be the same people who have cast doubt on the possibility of early and flourishing African civilisations, on whether or not it was African civilisation which gave birth to the Zimbabwe ruins! Such denials should always remain matters of the most profound indifference to us, since we have already made the point that in the nature of the 'us' and 'them' categories communicative equivalence between whites and blacks must, for the time being at least, be considered a prospective matter, a mere future possibility.

Contributions to Philosophical Anthropology

The statement may be made that contributions purporting to create an understanding of man's own image (anthropology) are broadly of two types. The first type are the unmistakeable brain-children of the naturalistic positivistic ethos of the Anglo-Saxon part of the world. The primary objection to these contributions is that of reductionism – namely, the reduction of the human person to those attributes, traits or what you will which are supposedly available to objective measurement. It will readily be appreciated that though these contributions are more sophisticated, they retain very strong family links with the earlier psychologies of the pioneers. It is, however, gratifying to note that in recent years there has been a visible emphasis away from preoccupations with method to grappling with the enigma that is the human person (Bugental, 1967).

The second type of contributions has come mainly from the continent of Europe and has been articulated in South Africa by Prof. B.F. Nel (1967) of Pretoria University. These contributions are characterised as existentialistic or phenomenological. Although method is not unduly enshrined, it is considered important to the extent that it may lead to a better understanding of the human person. The primary thrust in these contributions is that of totality or wholeness, not only of an individual but that of the existential situation in which he finds himself. Man is always in a situation. He is always in constant dialogue (relation) with his lived-space. According to Van den Berg (1953), the notion of dialogue is the cornerstone of phenomenological psychology. Nel (1967) has given sufficient attention to the differences between naturalistic and phenomenological anthropologies. These are not to be repeated here.

The question arises: Is there an African contribution to philosophical anthropology? The answer is a decided yes. African ontology (analysis and understanding of existence) was documented only recently (Tempels, 1959). Its actual lifespan remains undated. There appears to be no history of idealistic philosophy in Africa, no concerns about eschatology and/or transcendentalism. This last observation may be debatable. What is not controversial is that the philosophy of dialogue, relation, interdependence – the total existential situation – were the very stuff of life in African existence. This truth requires amplification.

A detailed account of African ontology is given by Tempels (1959). Senghor's brief characterisation of this ontology will suffice for present purposes:

Like others, more than others, he distinguishes the pebble from the plant, the plant from the animal, the animal from Man; but, once again, the accidents and appearances that differentiate these Kingdoms only illustrate different aspects of the same reality. This reality is being and it is life force. For the African, matter in the sense the Europeans understand it, is only a system of signs which translates the single reality of the Universe: being, which is spirit, which is life force. Thus, the whole universe appears as an infinitely small, and at the same time an infinitely large, network of life forces which emanate from God and end in God, who is the source of all life forces. It is he who vitalises and devitalises all other beings, all the other life forces. (1966: 4)

Central to African ontology is a recognition that in order to understand the status of an individual at any given time (be it in the areas of interpersonal relations, health or disease) attention should be directed at his existential situation in its totality. This means that the relationship among the interdependent vital forces (life forces), elders, ancestors and God have to be fully appreciated in each situation.

This totality of the individual's existential situation was to be understood in relation to two existential categories. These categories may be stated as those of vital force (spirit) hierarchy and interdependence. Vital forces were considered to be interdependent and of different potency. Africans recognised relation (dialogue) as being fundamental to existence – to being-in-the-world. Without elaborating, I would like to suggest that African ontology in its own right is a significant contribution to philosophical anthropology. Its primary focus is on the existential situation in its totality, on dialogue as the most fundamental existential category.

We said at an earlier stage that culture must always be considered an existential medium for the constituting of man–world relations. At this stage the point may be made that the 'theory of forces' as an ontology constituted for the African a backdrop against which variations of cultural mediums could be developed. Since there has been and is an African ontology which has created cultural variations, there appears to be no sound basis for scepticism with regard to the respectability and status of the concepts of Négritude and African personality as defined by us. There has undoubtedly been a black, or more specifically African, mode of being-in-the-world – of dialogue, of relating to the body, to objects, to others and to time and space.

One may observe that as a result of a number of historical (e.g. colonialism) and socio-cultural contingencies (e.g. the missionary effort) most of the valuable aspects of African ontology were undermined. The colonisers waged a total war on Négritude (African personality) mainly through the missionary thrust. When we look back at these developments we see Africa going through its own Dark Age. Now, in the seventies, Africa is going through its Renaissance – making its own contribution to world humanism. This development is of the utmost importance since it is becoming increasingly clear that Western civilisation has gone into a veritable crisis (Sorokin, 1941). The civilisations of the West are now approximating the cancerous decline stage of the Roman Empire. That this is the case is easily demonstrated by the decline in the integrative status of our environments, and the development of large-scale subcultures and countercultures.

A short digression intended to suggest further evidence in favour of the view that Western civilisation is now post-menopausal will not be inappropriate. Frankl (1965) in his three-dimensional ontology suggests that man may be characterised, inter alia, by his being soma, psyche and spirit (noetic dimension). He goes on to suggest that a great many people experience their lives as 'existential vacuums'. We need not go into the details of Frankl's formulations but make the additional observation that Van den Berg has added flesh to

Frankl's three-dimensional ontology, by suggesting convincingly that Western society in its preoccupation with the democratic imperative of equality has elevated mediocrity to the status of a norm and a virtue.

Coupled with this development has been the secularisation of life, which has been expressing itself most dramatically in the rejection of the spiritual dimension of existence, of ideals. During the Victorian era and beyond, the specific areas of anomic isolation (socially disapproved of) were sex and aggression. As a result of the then current social attitudes towards these expressive areas they tended to be repressed and thus constituted most of the unconscious material of the people of the times. These affective states have been released from their social anomic isolation after Freud and are progressively being replaced in the unconscious by the domain of spirituality. The domain of spirituality, of ideals and values, by being shifted into the unconscious is being deprived of its primary function in society, namely, that of being the fountainhead of human creativity. This development in itself is sufficient to support our view that Western civilisation is decadent and sterile. Something may yet come from the black world to inject new vitality into this beautiful post-menopausal old lady!

At this stage in our discussion, we may pose the following question: To what extent is African ontology still operative in the African mode of being-in-the-world? It has to be conceded that in addition to the possible pervasive influence of this ontology, there have been various group adaptational response patterns which may not be disregarded in any attempts at understanding the African personality (Négritude) and being-black-in-the-world. It will suffice to note that the question posed here will be dealt with in another section of this book. It seems to us that an understanding of African ontology is a requirement for the possible formulation of what it means to be black-in-the-world. The following concluding points may now be made.

First, it must be made clear that the concept of African personality as understood by blacks is synonymous with that of Négritude as formulated by Senghor. We should not be dragged into simplistic attempts to psychologise the concept. Its major focus and coverage is the black experience of being-in-the-world. Second, just as much as theology has until recently ignored the black experience in its major formulations, so has philosophical anthropology. If philosophical anthropology should make any claims to validity and universality, it will have to be reconsidered in the light of the black experience. Let it be so.

5 | Nausea

The fundamental subject of *The Myth of Sisyphus* is this:
it is legitimate and necessary to wonder whether life
has a meaning; therefore it is legitimate to meet the
problem of suicide face to face. The answer, underlying
and appearing through the paradoxes which cover it, is
this: even if one does not believe in God, suicide is not
legitimate.

Thus declared Camus, the philosopher-novelist of the absurd,
in 1955. A little later, he goes on to say:

There is but one serious philosophical problem
and that is suicide. Judging whether life is or is not
worth living amounts to answering the fundamental
question of philosophy. All the rest – whether or not
the world has three dimensions . . . comes afterwards.
(Camus, 1955: 3)

In more general terms, the fundamental problem posed by
Camus may be described as that of suffering. It is suffering in
the most general terms which results in 'nausea' and a sense of

the absurd. Let us, however, return to Camus for a disconcerting dramatisation of the absurdity of human existence:

> It happens that the stage sets collapse. Rising, streetcar, four hours in the office or the factory, meal, streetcar, four hours of work, meal, sleep and Monday Tuesday Wednesday Thursday Friday and Saturday according to the same rhythm – this path is easily followed most of the time. But one day the 'why' arises and everything begins in that weariness tinged with amazement. (1955: 19)

This sense of the absurd is what Frankl (1965) describes as the 'existential vacuum'. When the 'why' arises it becomes insistent, almost a compulsive neurosis. The answer to this 'why', as Camus and Frankl would tell us, takes various forms ranging from a mild sense of discomfort to psychopathological reactions and sometimes to contemplations of suicide. In this essay, I prefer to leave aside the more general problems of the absurdity of human existence in order that I may pay attention to some specific aspects. Here I wish to refer to that form of human suffering known as illness. It must be during those particularly solitary moments in the sickbed that the 'why' articulates itself with the force of a sledgehammer. Van den Berg (1966) gives us a vivid description of the meaning of being ill. The most dramatic changes in the life of the individual which occur as a result of a sudden onset of illness are those affecting his relationships with his body, objects, time, space and other people. The sick individual becomes estranged from his body and his environment. He tends to live more in the here and now than in terms of his past or his future. In terms of an individual's existential situation, these changes may be so all-encompassing that perplexity and despair may follow. Depending on one's socialisation, education, time perspective and premorbid status, the question 'why' is more likely to insinuate itself into one's stream of consciousness.

It has been known for a long time that the meaning of illness is, like other social reaction patterns, culturally determined. This truism also goes for the experience of pain. Sternbach (1968), for example, has suggested that pain has important interpersonal communication meanings for the patient. Cultural relativity with respect to pain and illness is understandable if we should concede that different cultural climates result in different patterns of relation to the body, to others, to objects and to space and time. These existential categories tend to constitute themselves in specific combinations which also determine the meaning of being ill. Some observers may argue that where organic pathology is demonstrable the probability of universal patterns of response is greater. It may well be that this is the case. This observation, however, would not go so far as to obscure the equally valid point that the subjective experience of the same organic process would be variant in different cultural settings. Some of the reasons for these variations should become clearer in due course.

There is one point which should be made at this stage. A consistent theme throughout this collection has been the conviction that there has been and is a distinct mode of being-black-in-the-world. It has also been shown that this mode of being-in-the-world may be characterised as being expressive of Négritude – of the African personality. The impression should be avoided that one is dealing with a static socio-cultural phenomenon. Instead, it should be emphasised that one is dealing with a dynamic process. It is for this reason that it was suggested that the second Renaissance may well emerge from the African continent.

Far-reaching changes are taking place on the African continent. These changes are a result of many cultural change agents such as urbanisation and industrialisation. Coupled with these are the changes which may be seen to be related to the emergence of many countries from the status of colonies to full sovereign status. The present century is possibly witnessing the last vestiges of the so-called 'traditional' societies in Africa (Gutkind, 1970). White observers have never tired of pointing out that there are several varieties of man in Africa, such as the 'attention-getting elites', the 'detribalised man', the 'transitional man' and the 'developing man'.

It is legitimate to observe that there is socio-cultural change in Africa. To say that the individuals exposed to such change are 'transitional' or 'developing' is highly questionable. This change only becomes transitional if one presupposes that the change will necessarily be in the direction of Western standards. This issue appears to be prejudged as far as the Western world is concerned. Since we are not bound to accept the enthusiasm of the West, we find ourselves compelled to ask: transitional or developing in relation to what standards? This remains an open question. We may now return to the question of illness, which we hope to discuss very briefly.

Let it be said that suffering, pain and illness as expressions of existential absurdity are a given of existence. They appear to be of the same status as time and space. Just as the constitution of space and time into lived-space is variable, so is the ontological interpretation of illness. We find on reflection that the status of being ill in the African is experienced as a state of incongruence (disharmony) between the individual and his fundamental transactions with his total existential situation.

This means that in order to appreciate the meaning of being ill one has to have an understanding of African ontology – the African's philosophy of being, his philosophy of existence. Reference has already been made to this ontology. It will suffice here to limit myself to the following additional observations.

African ontology conceives of reality as consisting of interacting, interdependent life forces. These life forces are not of the same magnitude. Depending on an individual's social and other circumstances, his life force (vital force) could be vitalised (increased) or devitalised (decreased). He could, as it were, be very well or ill. It is understandable why the aetiology and the possible treatment of an individual's illness must be searched for and understood in terms of his relations with other vital forces in his environment. Since we have admitted the existence of change in Africa an important question which arises and requires clarification is the following: Is African ontology still valid? Put differently: Could this ontology still be identified with being-black-in-the-world? When we look at the changes which are taking place in Africa we are forced to admit that this could not be an idle question. In order to decide whether this ontology is still a force to be reckoned with, we have to address ourselves to some sociological evidence. It is beyond the scope of this account to give a detailed discussion of this evidence. A brief reference will be made to the South African situation.

The social processes of urbanisation and industrialisation have been studied by several workers (Holleman *et al.*, 1964). Wilson (1964), reporting on her work in Langa (Cape Town), identified three groups: townsmen, migrants and the Iibari. She also found that there were distinct social groupings such as home-boy cliques, church groups, sporting clubs and savings societies (Wilson, 1964). The comprehensive studies by Mayer are referred to later in this book. One other notable feature about Africans in town is the fact that they live in African residential settings which according to Hellman (1971) may be considered to be satellite cities, such as Soweto (Johannesburg). The processes of urbanisation and industrialisation could not be considered significant in themselves without the additional influences of education and religion. One of the factors which suggest the possible significance of African ontology in the lives of millions of Africans today is the noted resilience of traditional beliefs in the areas of health and disease. This resilience is evidenced by the fact that Africans in South Africa and elsewhere may be classified into three categories on the basis of their response to available medical services. The first is the group of hidebound purists who will only use traditional African services and remedies. The second group consists of those Africans who use Western remedies and services to the total exclusion of traditional services. The third group consists of those Africans who tend to use a combination of traditional and Western services depending on circumstances.

In order to deal with our question more fully, it is necessary to understand the African's perception of being-in-the-world, his mode of experiencing his phenomenal self, his experience. An exercise of this kind leads one to recognise the current validity of African ontology as an organising force in the lives of the Red migrants, the Amaqaba and some townspeople. It appears reasonable to assume that in the lives of these people no subjective experience of being-in-the-world exists other than that organised around the theory of forces. There appears to be no possibility of a competing world view. If and when Western ideas are adhered to, they tend to be subjectively experienced within the framework of African ontology. The relationship involved is not one of conflict and contradiction, but one which is dialectical – a situational synthesis. What about the real townsmen? Why do we find that even in their case there is invariably a sporadic return to African ontology? This return is represented by the usual combination of traditional and Western remedies. In my view, this pattern of response is proportionately related to the degree of stress experienced by the individual and his family, since in our case illness is hardly ever an individual matter. Reflection tells us that in these situations we are dealing with competing ontologies – two world views. It is not difficult to recognise that African ontology has decided historico-cultural advantages over Western conceptions derived from the current dominant cultures.

Our analysis tells us further that explanations about the resilience of traditional beliefs which are based on the defence mechanism hypothesis – which understand the African's reaction as constituting a security operation – do not tell the whole story. It seems to me that while the principle of situational relevance accounts for a considerable part of the behaviour, it is necessary to suggest that African ontology as an organising force, though it may have become dissociated from the self-systems of many Africans, tends to remain latent as long as stress is subliminal, only to be activated the moment the stress is beyond a certain threshold.

It is now proper to return to the more general problem of suffering, of the absurdity of human existence, with which we started. I do not intend to spend a great deal of time on this problem. I would like to make a few concluding remarks. Having been a colonised people over several centuries, and still being in important aspects a colonised people, the question arises as to whether suffering and the general absurdity of life can have the same meaning for us as it may have for white people. Put differently, one may inquire whether when black people ask the question 'why' they do, in fact, ask the same question suggested by Camus. The difference between the two questions which may be asked appears to be of the following order.

The absurd man projected by Camus directs his question to existence (life), as it were, or perhaps to God. The black man, on the other hand, directs his question to life as imposed on him by the white man. In the case of the black man, it has been the white man who has systematically created the specific form of the black man's existential absurdity. A further difference has been that we have not had any difficulties in identifying the source of our nausea – of our suffering. We have been compelled to recognise that unlike the white man we live with the originators of our absurdity. The source of our suffering may be identified in the streets of Pretoria and Johannesburg. Should it surprise anybody that the problem of suicide recognised by Camus as the most important problem of philosophy should be recognised as a paltry matter by us? The fact of the matter is that we live suicide and are too involved in living to contemplate it.

6 | Reflections of a Black Clinician

This essay is in three parts. The first section deals with the body boundary experiences of a group of hospitalised African paraplegics and normal subjects. This part of the essay is an expanded revised version of a paper published in 1972 (Manganyi, 1972a). The second part of the essay deals with neurotic disorders and problems of psychotherapy (treatment). The third part considers the community mental health approach.

Reflections on the Body

The body image concept was first introduced into the literature mainly as a result of the contribution in the sixteenth century of the French physician-surgeon, Ambroise Paré, who had interested himself in phantom limb phenomena in amputees (Kolb, 1959). Benton (1959) elects Pierre Bonnier as the first worker to develop the concept of an organised perceptual model of the body. Since then, this concept has been defined and developed notably by Gertsmann (1958) and Schilder (1964).

In the most general terms, the body image may be described as an individual's internalised conception, experience and image of his physical self. Much later in the study of the body image, it became apparent that the experience of the body could be studied on the basis of its boundary (peripheral) characteristics (Fisher and Cleveland, 1968a). Workers in this latter mould conceive of the body as having boundary features which may be penetrable or non-penetrable. These boundary features are to be understood as relating to the distancing of stimuli in relation to the body. It was not long before these workers demonstrated the fact that body boundary characteristics were related to certain personality constellations and adjustment strategies.

Of more immediate concern was the recognition by several workers that the body image and its boundary features were extremely sensitive to early socialisation experiences (see, for example, Kolb, 1959; Witkin *et al.*, 1962; Fisher and Cleveland, 1968a). From this observation, it is not a long step to conclude that since socialisation experiences are culturally determined, such differences should account for some measure of difference in the development of body boundary features in different cultural settings. In recognition of this possibility, the present writer became interested in the probable influence of these pathoplastic factors (cultural) in the form assumed by body image disorders in an African group of subjects. This interest was expressed through the formulation of two research hypotheses.

First, the paraplegics as a clinical group would show evidence of disorder in their experience of their bodies (body image) when compared to a comparable group of non-hospitalised normal subjects. Second, the paraplegics would give evidence of a lifestyle characterised by a higher loading on passive-submission as opposed to active-coping when compared against a comparable group of non-hospitalised normal subjects. The method and statistical results of my interest in this problem are reflected in the original paper and will not be repeated here.

For the general reader, what is most important is a discussion of the findings of that small investigation. These results and the discussion will not be presented in their technical form. What is intended here is to give the reader a general feel of the subject. The major finding, a rather intriguing one, was that all the predictions which were made were not supported by the evidence of the study. What emerged was a compelling suggestion that both the sick subjects (paraplegics) *and* the non-impaired subjects revealed evidence of disturbances in the two areas investigated, namely, body image experience and lifestyle (self-steering).

At this stage in our discussion, it may be helpful to clarify the idea of self-steering behaviour as a lifestyle. The compound word 'self-steering' suggests the meaning: Self-steering individuals may be characterised as those who are adequate and competent in their transactions with their environments. This lifestyle has also been characterised as active-coping. On the other hand, there are in any society a group of inadequate individuals whose lifestyle may be described as being highlighted by passive-submission. These are the social malcontents who in the face of adversity give up hope and 'despair to drowning'.

Another idea which is worth clarifying is that of the condition of being paraplegic. Paraplegia may arise from an injury or a disease of the spinal cord. Injuries to the spinal cord resulting in a paralysis and sensory loss in the lower part of the body (depending on the level of the lesion) may occur as a result of industrial, home and road accidents. Crime also contributes its share to the number of people who are so inflicted. Besides the other physical complications and the usually long periods of immobilisation which are necessary, there are a number of psychic reaction patterns which have been identified (Beneš, 1968). Psychological adaptation in a paraplegic patient is said to progress through five stages. The first of these stages is related to the psychic trauma which later develops into a state of depression associated with a lack of mobility. The second stage consists of a lifting of the depression and general improvement related to optimism about recovery. The third stage is characterised by the development of complications and pain, which improve gradually. During the fourth stage, the patient experiences hours of depression with loss of self-esteem and despair. In the fifth and final phase the mental status of the patient becomes stabilised. Characteristic of this stage is a generalised loss of drive and interest in society. Neurotic behaviour patterns and recourse to alcohol and drugs are not uncommon at this stage.

It will be evident from this brief discussion that paraplegics are very sick people indeed. Evident also is the fact that these patients must experience a dramatic change in the images of their bodies in addition to the other psychic problems which have been listed above, chief among which is a generalised loss of drive and interest in society. I reported earlier that when paraplegic patients were compared with fully functioning individuals no statistically significant differences between the two groups were found. Instead, what emerged very distinctly was the fact that both groups experienced their bodies very diffusely (indefinite body boundaries) and had a lifestyle characterised by passive-submission and a chronic sense of helplessness in the face of environmental odds. I must say that I was alarmed by the ominous suggestions of these findings. This is why I decided to include this essay in this collection. In a treatment of this kind it is possible to reflect more freely on the findings' general implications than was the case in an academic thesis.

A finding which suggests a real possibility that there existed no difference in certain measures between a very sick group of patients and patently normal citizens can only generate concern in all people of goodwill. Intriguing as this finding may be, the more important question which follows relates to the possible origin of this status of being generally unwell in spite of all indications to the contrary. The actual psychological mechanisms which may be invoked to explain the status of these African groups are fairly complicated and will not be discussed in detail here. It will suffice to point out that body experience is intimately related to early socialisation and perceptual experiences. Let us deal with the body experience disorder revealed in these groups.

What in terms of the African experience of being-in-the-world does it mean to talk about the socialisation of the body image? It means, as was suggested earlier, that in the African experience there has over time developed a sociological schema of the black body prescribed by white standards. The prescribed attributes of this sociological schema have, as we should all know by now, been entirely negative. It should be considered natural under these circumstances for an individual black person to conceive of his body as something which is essentially undesirable (something unattractive), something which paradoxically must be kept at a distance, outside of one's self so to speak. This paradoxical feat is, of course, never achieved in reality. It expresses itself in reality in a sort of diffuse body experience, a certain inarticulateness of the experience of the physical self. Another trick, so often played on the black body, has been the attempt to impose certain attributes of the white body (appeal characteristics like skin colour and hair texture).

In spite of the costly effort expended by some individuals in this direction, it should never be expected that these external (to the black body) attributes would be integrated into the black body. Neither could the imposition of these attributes on the sociological schema of the black body be expected to drastically improve its status. These, I contend, are some of the factors responsible for the noted pathological experience of the black body.

What follows is worth repeating because it is of great importance. Black people the world over have to face the challenge of improving the socialisation of the black body. It is we who have to eradicate the negative sociological schema prescribed by whites. This might mean that some cosmetic empires might find themselves in the red. This certainly should be no dear concern of ours. There appears to be sufficient evidence for those prepared to see it that the black body can stand on its own without the sort of borrowing that has been going on for years.

A socio-cultural assault on the bodies of a whole people is perhaps one of the most vicious tragedies that can befall a people. This truth is simply illustrated. The physical body constitutes an individual's anchor in the world. It is the physical body which makes it possible for an individual to be given a name, to tell all and sundry who he is – to constitute lived-space. The body is the nexus of all the fundamental relations (dialogue) which an individual develops with others, with objects and with space and time. If the integrity of the body is violated, as it has been in the case of black people, the other existential relationships also become distorted. Integrity for the body is what a solid foundation means for a good house. Violate the integrity of this foundation (the body) and everything else collapses after the fact. Thus it is that we were forced to experience our bodies as though they were not ours, as though our bodies were prospective and were hiding from us in the white suburbs and cosmetic firms.

Another experience of the author may serve to illustrate the significance of the sociological schema a little further. Some unpublished data on African albinos in a Soweto school sample suggested tentative support for the view that a negative or an ambiguous sociological schema creates an essentially negative self-evaluation. A technique for the study of the body image was used to study this group which included a requirement for a self-portrait. When the data was analysed and compared with the other body image data, it was found that the albinos, unlike the control group of subjects, had a great deal of trouble creating a self-portrait, a fact which suggested the active intervention of negative self-evaluation ideation. My own experience in the field of the body has long led me to the conclusion that a socio-cultural assault on the body will require an equally wide-ranging offensive at the socio-cultural level.

Some observers may feel that this whole question about the black body having been abused in many more ways than one is nothing more than a storm in a teacup. Such detractions would not be entirely unexpected. Disregarding such frivolous claims, I continue to reflect on the condition of being-black-in-the-world. There is another side to the story about the socio-cultural assault on the black body which requires reflection. This reflection is intended to answer the following question: If, as we suggest, the black body has been forced into diffuseness and ambiguity, what were and are the related consequences?

One of the most important findings of body image studies is the following: It has been found, for example, that individuals with diffuse body boundaries tended to have a low aspiration level, to lack a sense of independence. In achieving societies, these individuals could not be anything but failures of one type or another. In part, this general finding explains the experience of an almost malignant sense of helplessness which was observed in the groups which I studied. Perhaps it must be added that in the African experience there are other considerations which should always be kept in mind. Outside the distortions of relationships which have been associated with the negative sociological schema of the black body there have been other unfavourable experiences.

Why should black people experience such a sense of insecurity and crippling despair? White observers are known to believe that this sense of insecurity is a general human condition which may become acute during periods of mass stresses and strains such as are involved in urbanisation and industrialisation. Our own view is that while this may be true, it may well be that there are quantitative and qualitative differences in the experience of existential stress. The fundamental difference, as I said elsewhere, is that the slave does not or, better still, cannot experience the absurdity of his existence as being a condition of life. He rather experiences it as arising out of the condition of being a slave. Among other things, the condition of being a slave means that one is too tied up with the actual business of living, of planning for tomorrow's supper, to be concerned about the so-called terrifying freedom of individual existence. For a man whose existential alternatives are so limited from birth, freedom, like eternal life, can only assume the status of a catchword. The idea of existential alternatives also involves that of personal growth, of self-realisation. We as black people have been living on deficiency motivation, on the motivation of want. To grow in stature as a people would have been a contradiction of motivation theory.

We find, therefore, that while the white man is exploring the moon, the black man, deprived of all active participation in the history of man, is still suffering from the onslaughts on his body. With limited existential alternatives he trades on the motivation of want. Could it be that we are doomed to perpetual servitude? That will be the day!

Reflections on the Psychiatric Patient

In 1970 I reported a number of case histories of psychiatric patients seen at Baragwanath Hospital in Johannesburg. Since that time I have seen many more patients. The clinical presentations have been many and varied, representing a broad spectrum of all known psychiatric disorders. Acute and episodic psychotic confusional states, usually of obscure origin, are not uncommon. So is the condition known as schizophrenia. Neurotic disorders, usually with physical equivalents, are probably on the increase. Among the commonest of these disorders are the anxiety states, usually with reactive depression components. Conversion reactions with coexisting anxiety are also common.

The neuroses are indeed no longer the diseases of the wealthy. This recognition immediately poses a number of problems. There is the question of treatment (psychotherapy). Africans have been practising some form of supportive helping for several centuries. Psychotherapy as currently practised by professionals is as yet unknown in the African community. Some observers have used this fact as an excuse for providing the most rudimentary of psychiatric services. Others have contended that since psychotherapy is not of the African culture, it will remain unacceptable to Africans of all descriptions. But this sort of argument does not hold any water, since it could also be argued that modern methods of contraception are foreign to the African experience.

These diversionary tactics must be taken for what they are. I know of no group in the world which has accepted medical advances of any kind without some cold reserve. That this is so is evidenced by the always present need for public health education. Public education for mental health among Africans will present its own problems, but so does public health education on family planning. If only Africans could be taught to have smaller but psychiatrically unhealthy families: That would be a satisfactory state of affairs! The conviction is strong that the present evidence in the mental health sphere does not in any way justify the extent of public social neglect in so vital an area of our existence. Before discussing mental health in general, it is necessary to return briefly to the problem of the treatment of psychiatric disorders among Africans.

The psychiatric patient presents himself to the doctor, let us say a psychiatrist or a clinical psychologist. In this case, the patient is likely to have been referred by a physician who will have satisfied himself that the patient is not afflicted with an essentially organic (physical) illness. Since there are no black psychiatrists in South Africa today, such a patient tends to be a professional nuisance to the white psychiatrist or clinical psychologist. For a start, there is the problem of communication, which for purposes of psychotherapy is insurmountable. In this situation, the psychiatrist can only hope to have the faintest of ideas with respect to the problems the patient might be having. In some situations the psychiatrist's difficulty may be alleviated by the fact that the patient may be an educated black who may be fluent in more languages than his mother tongue. Other difficulties arise in such cases. Usually, the black patient is hardly ever free to look at the doctor as simply a doctor.

The doctor remains, in the experience of the black patient, a white doctor. This qualification is of the utmost importance, since it carries so much of the behaviour which goes on below the verbal level. For the doctor the situation is also not simple, because he too is involved in a relationship not with a patient but with a black patient – a qualification that is equally important.

Those who may doubt the validity of these observations may only be doubting my good faith, for I have had the experience of patients saying 'Baas' and 'Master' to white doctors. Never have I come across any doctor who appeared shocked by this scandalous suggestion!

I think it is probably important to make the point that the psychiatric patient presents special problems in view of the fact that the nature of the patient–doctor relationship is crucial. In this case the total communication milieu is of such importance. It is well known that communication between two individuals who may be from the same cultural backgrounds and who use the same language forms may be a complicated affair. In ordinary circumstances, 'vocal' communication as opposed to 'verbal' communication would involve such things as tone of voice, gesture and facial expression. This means that the communicative act may be very refined and subtle, to the extent that if one is not listening with the 'third ear' one may miss the import of the message.

There has been a previous reference to the unique South African communication problems. This may now be taken a step further by pointing out a few more interesting aspects of the matter. I am not in any way scapegoating the black body. This point has to be made. It was suggested during an earlier analysis that the body in its sociological schema may relate on the basis of its appeal or barrier attributes. This suggests that the body is in a very real sense a medium for distancing. This attribute of the body is maximally expressed in the attraction or repulsion between people of the two sexes. The issue we are dealing with now amounts to the question of whether the black body is, in interracial communication, an asset to effective communication or not. One cannot escape the feeling that in such situations the black body would tend to create distance because of its barrier characteristics. This means, in effect, that even before communication refinements such as tone and gesture are introduced into the communication mix, the message (or rather one of the messages) has been grossly communicated through the body. It is as though the body has said to the white doctor or psychiatrist: Keep your distance, I am black!

If there should be any grain of truth in what I have been saying, some objections which may be raised must be dealt with immediately. For example, the question may legitimately be asked of whether I am suggesting that blacks and whites never really talk to each other. Such an interpretation would be to simplify the issue beyond recognition. My reaction would be to say that blacks and whites talk down and up to each other. This is another way of saying that what seems to do the talking in the white person is the master and what does the responding in the black man is the servant. In practical terms this has meant that white people always experience themselves as communicating instructions, even if this appears otherwise in any specific situation. The black person has tended to communicate an apology, not for any conceivable palpable reason. One instructs, the other apologises!

All that has been said suggests that to talk about dialogue where there is no significant possibility of healthy relating is to indulge in sophistry of the worst kind. Relating in the sense of both narrowing the distance and sharing in the sense of experiencing the world as our-world is imperative for effective communication. This is not likely to be achieved in our lifetime. Thus we find that the doctor and his patient, the manager and his worker, are all back at square one. There is a definite impasse which will require all the goodwill in the world to overcome.

I have deliberately left out of this discussion the actual difficulties experienced in psychotherapy with African patients because I have dealt with these elsewhere (see Manganyi, 1972b). From what has been stated above it should be clear that the treatment of black patients by white psychiatrists is fraught with immense difficulties. At this point it may be stated that, obvious as it may sound, the best hope lies, for the time being at least, in the training of black clinicians.

Reflections on Community Mental Health

The first two sections of this essay have highlighted the existence of psychiatric and other emotional disturbances which are part and parcel of the black experience in South Africa. The problem of treatment, particularly of neurotic disorders, is not limited to the individual patient but raises the further question of available strategies to deal with mental disorders in the black communities. A meaningful way of reflecting on this subject is to begin, in this third section, by discussing some important general considerations as a framework for a more focused treatment.

To what extent does our environment as a totality facilitate or militate against the flourishing of positive mental health in the different population groups? This issue constitutes an inquiry into the integrative status of South African society. How does one judge the integrative status of a society? The answer to this question is provided by Leighton and Leighton, who observe as follows:

> To find where a community belongs on this range, one may use various sociocultural indicators: the poverty-affluence dimension; the overall coherence or confusion of cultural values; the vailability [sic] of its religious system; the stability of families; the leadership and followership; communication networks; supportiveness of interpersonal relationships ... the findings both in the Stirling County and among the Yoruba supported the hypothesis to the extent that mental health was considerably better in the integrated than the disintegrated communities. A corrollary [sic] of this hypothesis is that if the integrative status of a community improves, so will its mental health. (1967: 1532)

Langner and Michael (1963) have made a related observation, pointing out that with an increase in the number of unfavourable social experiences there is an associated increase of poor mental health. If one were to go by the occasional reports in the local press with respect to such socially pathological phenomena as crime, alcoholism, divorce and drug abuse, one would be inclined to doubt the integrative status of South African society as a whole. The situation is made more intolerable by the fact that there are in South Africa populations which are at special risk. These are the black South Africans (Africans, Indians and Coloureds). I say that they are populations at special risk in view of the fact that they have always been afflicted with a progressive accumulation of unfavourable social experiences associated with discriminatory legislation and practice. This is so true that Mayer (1972) could go as far as to describe the status of Africans in South Africa as pariah status, that experience of being insignificant.

It may easily be demonstrated that some of the mental health problems are strictly speaking unique to specific population groups, since they are a direct result of the current government posture: the posture of the now dominant white culture. An example a little later will demonstrate that this is true. There can be no argument about the fact that if judged by the sensible criteria suggested above, the integrative status of South African society must be very low indeed. The black communities must continue to be considered communities at special risk because it is in these communities where poverty and starvation are rife, where there is the greatest organised disruption of family life and an associated decrease in the number of supportive interpersonal relationships. In such disintegrating communities there can be no reasonable doubt about the existence of confusion with respect to cultural values.

An authentic case history will illustrate dramatically the differential effects of the posture of the now dominant white culture. In 1970, a woman aged 35 was referred to the Baragwanath Hospital psychiatric outpatients' department. She presented at that stage with the following complaints: She told us that she had developed a generalised loss of drive and concentration and that her work as a midwife had become shoddy. Detailed physical examinations by the physicians had failed to reveal any physical pathology. Psychiatric examination, on the other hand, revealed that a diagnosis of reactive depression could confidently be arrived at.

Her personal history revealed a number of special difficulties. She had been divorced and had been granted custody of their five minor children. After the divorce, she was compelled by law to vacate the house in which the family had been living. Attempts to secure alternative housing had been fruitless and she found herself compelled to live with an elder sister, who also had children of her own, in a three-roomed house. We understood her reactive depression to represent the response of a divorced mother to a number of unfavourable life experiences.

Adequate psychiatric intervention would have meant not only giving her medication and psychotherapy but also a much needed restructuring of her social conditions. Psychiatry is not expected to supply husbands where these are not available. Improvement of her social conditions would have meant that she should have found it possible to work and bring up her children as ideally as was within her means. She had, in effect, been given this responsibility by the law. In this particular case psychiatry found itself helpless because her social conditions were so inflexible (could not be changed), since they were prescribed by the 'South African way of life'. With patients of this kind and many others, it must be admitted that they will not be helped by whatever rudimentary psychiatric services may be in existence.

The tragedy assumes its proper dimensions once it is recognised that current estimates show, for example, that there are 13 000 families on the waiting list for family housing. What of the divorcees, the single women with illegitimate children? There must literally be thousands of these people in Soweto and elsewhere who have no recourse to the benefits of psychiatry.

Lay opinion would have us believe that the neuroses are essentially a social class disease. In a sense this may be so. Their nuisance value may be related to social status, but they have been found to exist even in rural African communities. Support for this last statement emerges from the now fairly well-described hysterical manifestations in rural African communities identified as Ufufunyane by the Zulu and Ukuphosela by the Xhosa. The nuisance value of the psychoses has ensured that various institutions be created for custodial care and treatment. Facilities for the treatment of the psychoneuroses are virtually non-existent outside the occasional outpatients' clinics, which have so many problems that they are not as useful as they otherwise could have been.

The question may now be posed as to whether, in fact, there is anything which may be done to restore positive mental health as a major socio-political priority to its rightful place in our society. Since a great deal of our mental health problems (especially differential expressivity) must be considered related to the posture of the dominant white culture, particularly in its political expression, it must be conceded that the primary prevention solution may only be initiated at that level. That government action in the mental health sphere is imperative was demonstrated by the American Congress. In a historic move, the American Congress debated and passed Federal Legislation P.L. 88-164: the Community Mental Health Act of 1963. Since that legislation, it has been estimated that by the year 1980, 2 000 community mental health centres will have been established throughout the country (Caplan, 1970).

The most important features of the community mental health approach are the following: There is the creation of community mental health centres in the various communities where the need is greatest. There is a constant monitoring of communities at special risk. These centres are expected to provide inpatient facilities, outpatient care, facilities for partial hospitalisation and emergency services, as well as facilities for public education and mental health consultation. One of the hallmarks of community mental health has been its lively interest in prevention. Prevention may be primary, secondary or tertiary. Primary prevention is directed at the reduction of new cases of mental disorder in communities through the planned elimination of pathogenic factors in those environments in addition to educational strategies directed at increasing the potential of individuals to deal with stress. Secondary prevention is intended to reduce the incidence of mental disorders as a result of early identification and immediate effective treatment. Tertiary prevention is directed at the elimination of 'residual disability' resulting from mental disorder as well as the provision of necessary follow-up care for those patient populations. Crisis intervention-oriented treatment modalities have been developed and are in current application. These methods are supplemented by the availability of mental health consultation services. Consultation skills are offered to other caregiving agencies in the community and they provide follow-up care and feedback to the community mental health centres.

It seems to me that mental health problems may be tackled at two possible levels. The first level of attack, namely, the attack at the level of the state, we could characterise as the primary level of attack. The second level is the secondary level, about which I have a few things to say.

Most important, it is a shame for an advanced country such as ours not to have a single black psychiatrist, not even in exile. Usual explanations such as those advanced for the shortage of medical personnel are unsatisfactory in the face of the health problem. We leave aside such bickering and concentrate on the problem at hand, namely, the problem of what may yet be done at the secondary level of solution. An important strategy for adoption is the 'gem' of community mental health: mental health consultation. Let us describe this strategy briefly and then go on to suggest how it can find beneficial application in our society. Mental health consultation is today one of the most significant developments in the history of comprehensive community mental health. As technique and method, it arose out of a crisis. In the United States it developed from the realisation that mental health professionals in relation to the needs of communities would always be in short supply. Mental health consultation may briefly be defined as an interaction between a mental health consultant and a client. The consultant is a specialist in the mental health field and helps consultees in the solution of specific problems and/or increasing their skills in handling such problems.

The characteristic emphasis of mental health consultation is on prevention (in all its forms), environmental manipulation, early case detection, early crisis intervention and a decided emphasis on brief, effective contacts. Mental health consultation is geared towards the solution of specific problem(s). Since problems in mental health are many and varied, it follows that mental health consultation must be characterised by flexibility.

The effective use of mental health consultation skills depends in large measure on the studied isolation of points of entry into communities. These entry points consist of those individuals and agencies that make the utmost contact with individuals in the community: the clergy, general practitioners, social welfare workers, public health nurses, guidance and counselling personnel in schools and universities where such workers exist, and human relations workers in commerce and industry. Mental health consultation with respect to these groups would consist of organised efforts at increasing their skills in the mental health field. This may be achieved, inter alia, through seminars, workshops and individual training. Besides offering help to people in distress, they could act as sensitive observers and could be of great help in the early detection of mental and emotional disorders. Mental health consultation is particularly germane to our local situation with its noted scarcity of mental health professionals. This appears to be the strategy for adoption.

However, I do think that it must be emphasised that mental health problems should be tackled at the primary level. This demands a serious assessment of our socio-political fabric to determine in what ways improvements could be made to heighten the integrative status of our society. In the African communities, for example, efforts could be made to deal with the socially and psychologically disruptive effects of the migratory labour system. There are many other areas centred around discriminatory practices which could be handled. For the present, our biggest hope lies in the active promotion of mental health consultation practice. The limited professional skills which exist in this country may be used to man consultation services for the various population entry points.

I would like to refer in particular to several target groups which I consider vital in our situation. Commerce and industry may become important mental health agents by being more sensitive to the quality of life of their employees. This objective may be achieved broadly in the following way: Organisations could be more concerned about organisational hygiene in the area of industrial relations. Personnel functions, for example, may be arranged in such a way as to include some mental health structures in their primary areas of competence. Priorities for the training of industrial mental health workers (counsellors) could be worked out to suit local conditions. American experience in industrial counselling could prove invaluable. During the early stages of this development, industry and commerce could very well rely on consultative services while making use of domestic mental health workers to take care of employees in distress. In this way, industry and commerce could realise an important prevention function: the early identification of mental disorder and crisis intervention. Mental health consultation could be practised here on a large scale.

It will not be necessary to formulate in detail what other areas could be activated along the lines outlined above. It will be sufficient to indicate that entry points into communities could be developed based on mental health consultation principles. For special mention is the following observation: The creation of counselling and psychiatric facilities for Soweto, for example, is long overdue. Here then is a fertile area for social action. The churches and other organisations of goodwill could realise in a very concrete way their secular responsibilities by committing themselves to the creation of such facilities. Symbolic acts, however well intended they may be, will not in themselves be relevant to the lives of millions of blacks living in this country.

Some remarks on the responsibilities of our academic institutions will not be out of place. I would like to suggest some broad possibilities, based on the prerequisite of the active propagation of community mental health concepts in our universities, hospitals and clinics and in commerce and industry. It means in effect that mental health professionals and academics must begin to define their community responsibilities in terms of community needs rather than of their professional needs. The following suggestions may now be made:

1. Professional training in psychiatry and related professions should be restructured in such a way that practitioners are oriented away from the private (office) practice model to community mental health practice. Emphasis should be placed on the development of skills in community

consultation, programme evaluation and team approaches to therapy.

2. Particular attention should be paid to the training of non-traditional mental health caregivers. This is all the more imperative in view of the fact that experience elsewhere has demonstrated the impossibility of training sufficient numbers of clinical psychologists and psychiatrists to meet community needs.

3. There is a very strong case to be made for the restructuring of the training of social workers in our schools of social work. Psychiatric social work should be actively encouraged and taught. This would help augment the currently inadequate clinical skills.

4. Under current conditions in the black communities, the best hope lies in primary and secondary prevention strategies. These should be accompanied by a concerted effort in the direction of decentralisation of available psychiatric services. General hospitals and polyclinics should have primary psychiatric responsibilities all geared towards crisis intervention and a speedy return to the community.

Beyond doubt, the American experience in mental health is an invaluable source for South Africa. The relevance of that experience to our local conditions cannot be overemphasised.

7 | The Meaning of Change

During the year 1972, there was a great deal of noise here and abroad about what some people considered to be indications of change in the 'South African way of life'. It was suggested that these pointers of change could be identified in the political and economic spheres. Examples of this change were given. Following the Polaroid troubles, two big banking houses decided to 'equalise' salaries of blacks and whites.[1] There were public demands for a general narrowing of the wage gap as well as the organisation of black labour into trade unions. On the political front, people were saying that there was a need for 'dialogue' with the black communities. Some observers also suggested that the South African government was revealing a

---

[1] 'Caroline Hunter, co-founder of the Polaroid Workers Revolutionary Movement . . . stumbled upon evidence that her employer was providing the camera system to the South African state to produce photographs for the infamous passbooks for black residents. Hunter and her late husband, Ken Williams, then launched a boycott of the company. The boycott and divestment campaign ultimately grew to target other corporations in apartheid South Africa, including General Motors and Barclays Bank, among others. By 1977, Polaroid finally withdrew from South Africa' (Democracy Now, 2013).

more mature attitude towards the Buthelezis. Others observed that the Afrikaner was beginning to show some restlessness and was becoming more open and critical about the national policies of his government. When one looks back at all those 'happenings' one begins to wonder whether this change was apparent or real. Can it be truly said that South African society is changing? If this is so, what may be identified as the particular direction and form of this change? And would black and white South Africans be able to reach common agreement on the possible significance of this change? This essay concerns itself with these questions since we consider it necessary to achieve a black perspective (interpretation) on them.

We begin our analysis by borrowing some of the refreshing ideas of Prof. J.H. Moolman (1972), director of the African Institute in Pretoria. In spite of the unacceptability of some of his views, it should be admitted that he is an outstanding academic. One of his latest suggestions is that the Republic of South Africa should be viewed as a spatial system. He points out that this spatial system 'consists mainly of a white and black component'. Recognition is given to the fact that the white component is the dominant one in the system. Into the total spatial system was introduced the policy of separate development which has given birth to the concepts of 'homelands' and 'national units', which are now subsystems in the total spatial system. Some observations relating to these views may now be made. It should be pointed out that the fact that the white component is the dominant one in spite of being a minority group is very important. Important also is the fact that the policy of separate development which is creating new subsystems was imposed on the black component of the spatial system by the white component. Other issues pertinent to the views of Moolman will be raised later in this discussion. Let us return to the question of change in South Africa.

With respect to possible change in the spatial system it becomes interesting to reflect on the possible sources of change. On reflection one immediately recognises several possibilities. The most logical source of change is the white component of the spatial system. Since it is the dominant one, it may introduce new inputs into the system. This is precisely what it did when it imposed the policy of separate development on the black component, which created the Mangopes and the Matanzimas.[2] It is well known that the black component of the system had no active participation in the initiation of the new subsystems created by the policy of separate development.

Theoretically, the other source of change in the system is the black component. I say theoretically because it is a subordinate component. In spite of its current status in the spatial system, the possibility of its actively and directly introducing changes in the system may not be ruled out. New inputs into the system, insignificant as they may appear, are the recent development of Black Consciousness and solidarity, concepts which are threatening to undermine the subsystems created by the policy of separate development.

In considering the possible new inputs into the boundaries of the spatial system we must recognise that it is the black and white components of the system which may become change agents. The question arises at this stage of whether there are other possibilities which may introduce inputs into the main system while remaining essentially autonomous of the black and white components. In this category may be lumped such

---

[2] Lucas Mangope was the president of the Bantustan, or homeland, of Bophuthatswana, which was declared independent in 1977 by the apartheid government. Kaiser Matanzima was president of the Bantustan of Transkei, which the apartheid government declared independent in 1976.

forces as world hostility and opinion against current South African policies. Economic forces may also be included in this group. There can be no doubt about the fact that these forces are introducing inputs into the system. This admission does not amount to a recognition of these inputs as being decisive in changing the national character of South African life.

When one looks at the changes arising out of the dominant component, one recognises progression rather than a definite change in direction. This is easily shown to be the case since discriminatory legislation is the stock-in-trade of South African legislation. Voting patterns also show no significant swing to the left. There are several indications of social inertia in the dominant component which are expressed through current policies. One of these indications is the determination of the South African government to abide by the land allocation of a 1936 determination in spite of contraindications suggested by projected population statistics. Another indication of social inertia is the creation of the homelands. In this instance, it may be pointed out that the imposition of tribalism on the black component is a retrogressive step since black people are progressively going to reject tribalism as a basis for nationalisms. Job reservation provides additional evidence of the white component's reluctance to change with the times. It has been indicated that job policies are wreaking havoc with the economy. Even laypeople have begun to understand this situation and yet nothing of significance in this respect has been done. The catalogue could be developed further. We will return to this component a little later.

The black component is the subordinate one in the system. Does this in itself suggest that it is passive? This is definitely not the case. There are two considerations which are against this possibility. The first is the mere fact of it being the second main component in the system – its mere presence in the system. It thereby demands recognition from the dominant component. The second consideration is that, in terms of sheer numbers, it commands the majority while the dominant system constitutes a minority. This situation must be recognised as one which creates permanent tension in the spatial system. The black component is indirectly a change agent mainly because of its tension-creating potential. Outside these considerations, it may be stated that there are sporadic indications that the black component may progressively increase its tension-creating potential. Indications of this fact are the occasional 'illegal' strikes, and the development of Black Consciousness and of solidarity as organising concepts. One may recognise that in its tension-creating potential, the black component is currently characterised by the development of two subsystems. These spatial subsystems are represented by the increasingly articulate urban population and the homeland governments. There can be no doubt that these subsystems will continue to make demands (often conflicting ones) on the dominant white component.

Present indications are that the black component may in future introduce inputs (impose change) on the main system simply because of the fact that black people constitute the bulk of the labouring people of this country. Inputs may be introduced into the system, for example, once the black people recognise the significance of their increasing buying power. They may then decide to use this power for leverage in creating changes in the main system. Similarly, black labour may begin to exert its latent bargaining power (see discussion on this in Randall [1972], for example pages 55 and 87).

We said that changes may occur in the system as a result of forces originating from world opinion and economic considerations. These, as we may see later, are very closely related types of change agent. World opinion with respect to the policies of the South African government is no longer a monopoly of the United Nations and the Organisation for African Unity. Hostility against the policies of this country (the white component) has been expressed to the consternation and surprise of some Christians by such bodies as the World Council of Churches. Other anti-apartheid groups are in existence in several of the capitals of the Western world. The cumulative effect of this effort has been so wide that even the once benign Lesotho government has begun to hammer at our policies. ('Our policies' is naturally a speech habit more than anything else!) One may now ponder over the implications for change involved in this tension between South Africa and other world bodies. It should be admitted at the outset that one may only talk in terms of probability rather than fact in so complex an area of international and other relations.

These pressures will likely increase, as suggested by the recent change of attitude expressed by the new Australian government.[3] It is true to say that there are people who are revolted by current South African policies. With this recognition must come an awareness of the paradoxical nature of the situation, which presents itself in the following manner: There is sufficient evidence of big financial investment in the South African economy by the major powers of the West. While this is true, the people who would like to see changes in the

---

[3] In December 1972, the Australian Labor Party was elected into government. Led by Gough Whitlam, the new government changed its foreign policies and adopted a strong anti-racist stance against South Africa, which included sanctions and sport boycotts. Prior to this, the Australian government had had a long history of supporting white minority rule in southern Africa.

'South African way of life' are citizens of those countries which have a substantial stake in the future of this country. One must assume that their interest in our problems stems from motives of a much higher order, since this is the only way of resolving the paradox. For our own part we can only say that the black component must recognise that the dominant status of the white component is maintained and supported by inputs external to itself, namely, the large investments of the money giants of the twentieth century. This must mean that the black component has to realise that the fight for self-betterment may be understood as one which not only is essentially against the dominant white component but also involves the inputs of factors outside the main system.

We are often told that economic pressures at home will lead to domestic initiatives for change. This may well be. In this respect it should be made clear that we as black South Africans should never be deluded into believing that white South Africa is changing the moment we come across some symbolic acts like increases in salaries. These acts represent objective good (the moral sense), but should not be mistaken for a change of heart on the part of white South Africans. I may be taken to task for looking a gift horse in the mouth, but I would like to support my contention immediately. These acts are of a morally questionable character, since we know that they are not dictated by a sense of the moral and just. We know that they are not inspired by human decency – they do not spring from conviction. How do I defend such an allegation? I would like to say that it is because white people love themselves and the life they are leading that they find themselves forced to introduce some changes into the system. It is merely a question of self-love and self-interest. This view is supported by the fact that the suggested changes in the economic sphere arise out of the crisis in the economy and not from the suffering of black South Africans. This means that these changes, whenever they occur, should be viewed as being external to the white component of the system – as being something which has gone out of control. These observations suggest that some of the changes which will occur in the South African system will consist of these unplanned inputs. (Similar considerations are explored in Randall [1971].)

An important issue which should receive consideration is whether there can be any common agreement between the black and white components on the meaning of change in this country. This, at this stage in our history, is completely out of the question. We should not be shocked by the implications of this submission. Disagreement arises because white South Africans will always identify change which arises from unplanned inputs as being expressive of their own sense of justice. Since change in the direction of justice is foreign to the South African system, any triviality is likely to appear as something which is epoch-making. I once listened to a white South African tell an international conference in New York that he had succeeded in persuading industrial and commercial organisations to stop calling their employees 'boys'. This may be commendable, but what shocked me was that he reported this with so much enthusiasm and gratification that to him it must have been something deserving of a Nobel Prize.

Our response to tokens and symbolic acts must always accommodate a recognition that the interest of white South Africans in the plight of black South Africans may only be of a very superficial kind. This is related to the fact that they have no direct share in the black experience. It is also related to the fact that this interest may be purely self-reflexive, by which I mean to suggest that the interest stems from the white people's preoccupation with security: their own security. I am suggesting, in fact, that change in the South African spatial system is not likely to come from the white component. Such a possibility would be extremely paradoxical because it would involve a lot of altruism of a kind lacking in South African society. Since the dominant component is unlikely to introduce changes meaningful to the black component, most of the change which may overtake South African society may be of the unplanned variety. The usual references to revolution as against evolution as a possibility in South African society apply to these types of unplanned inputs.

I would like to end on the following note: In the abstract of Prof. Moolman's paper, the following important conclusion about the 'spatial system RSA' is arrived at:

The formation of sub-systems: a concept based on the premise that it is impossible – or at any rate undesirable – to attempt to break up the system into independent systems and that sub-systems should rather be formed: a reflection or microcosm, as it were, of the main system but retaining numerous characteristics of the main system such as territorial distinctiveness, (sub-) independence, a (sub-) economy and a specific nation as the nucleus nation and chief cohesive factor. The sub-systems approach is an acknowledgement of the cohesive force of uniformity in respect of culture, language, etc. At the same time, however, it is an acknowledgement of the fact that each distinctive nation in South Africa cannot exert its nationalism without restraint but is subject to necessary sacrifices by virtue of the multinational character of the system and the imperative need for a sub-system status. Those

who believe that separation between white and black
nations can be pursued to the full consequences of
sovereign independence subscribe to an illusion which
does not accord with the realities of the spatial system
RSA. (1972: 417)

Moolman's conviction about the spatial system RSA in relation
to the possible complete break-up of the spatial system into
black and white sovereign independent states is clear from
his last sentence. It seems, therefore, that we must recognise
that the spatial system RSA will have to retain unity at certain
levels. I would venture to suggest that peaceful coexistence in
this system and its subsystems will exist in proportion to the
amount of meaningful planned change which is introduced
into the system. For change to be meaningful, it will have to
be meaningful to both the black and the white components of
the system. In the meantime, we will have to keep a vigil of an
unknown duration, since meaningful change has not yet made
an appearance on the South African horizon (compare Khoapa
[1972: 67] in a text edited by Steve Biko).[4]

---

[4] The Publications Control Board redacted text in the original version of this
note. This reflects the practices of the time. *Black Viewpoint* – with contributions from Njabulo Ndebele, C.M.C. Ndamse, Chief M.G. Buthelezi and
Benny A. Khoapa – was edited by Stephen Biko and published by Spro-Cas in
1972. Biko was banned in 1973, the same year that *Being-Black-in-the-World*
was published, and Biko's involvement likely caused the security police to
instruct the Board to redact the information. It has not been possible to trace
the unredacted text.

8 | *Postscriptum* – 'African Time'

This is indeed an afterthought. My thoughts had actually wandered off the subject matter of the essays which I had just completed, and I had started working in my study on the problem of identity. While reflecting on this difficult subject, I remembered that a friend had recounted how he had been shocked by the contents of a recent publication. I also remembered that he had been indignant and amazed that such ideas could still find their way into academic print. I know him to be a very balanced person who is never overhasty with opinions. Since I had just been working on some aspects of the African experience, my curiosity was naturally aroused by this bit of information.

With unusual curiosity, I instituted an immediate search for 'Tyd en Neurose by die Bantoe', translated in the summary as 'The Bantu, Time and Neuroses' (Engelbrecht, 1972). For the benefit of those readers who may be unable to consult the original, I would like to quote two paragraphs from the English summary which represent the main theses of the paper. Prof. Engelbrecht writes as follows:

> The tempo of life of the Bantu is slow – slower than that of the white. You can see a different time in their

bodily movements, in the things of their world, in their places, in the whole landscape in which they exist. There is a remarkable difference between the lived-time (vital time) of the white and the black. We find two different tempos in two different worlds. When these two different worlds and realities come into contact, distortion and dislocation of human time takes place. Since time is a fundamental dimension of human existence the total existential situation of the individual and society will also be affected and distorted.

The life-world of the Bantu is totally different from that of the white. Integration and equation would not only create confusion but also psychological and social disturbances. On the other hand, the tempo of life of the Bantu is perhaps too slow for a too rapid development and change. (1972: 2)

I would like to be arrogant enough to take this celebrity of philosophy at the University of the North to task for some of his unfounded claims. My primary intention is to demonstrate briefly that his paper is in essence an apology for separate development. The writer's assurance that he is not interested in political controversy is indeed a red herring. Let me avail myself of the opportunity of saying that Prof. Engelbrecht is interesting himself in highly important but difficult problems. Let me say also that the bibliographical notes in his paper are very impressive. He definitely keeps excellent company! Perhaps I should add that he is a philosopher. I had really not been aware that he is interested in psychiatry and psychology. Being a philosopher, his interest in matters psychological is perhaps understandable. Small wonder that he writes with the calm conviction of a master. In spite of all these considerations, I wondered as I read through his paper whether he had not ventured too far afield. Of course, this is debatable. This possible debate is easily settled. I am a black clinician, by which I do not wish to suggest a monopoly of knowledge in this area. I simply have both an academic and existential advantage over Prof. Engelbrecht because I am part of the experience which he has been trying to understand from his office desk or his car.

Let me say at this stage that my essays, which were prepared before my familiarity with Prof. Engelbrecht's contribution, deal with some of the main issues raised in his paper. This amounts to saying that I am the first person to agree with the view that there is a black mode of being-in-the-world. This theme runs through my essays. This should be considered the only point of agreement between myself and Prof. Engelbrecht.

To return to his analysis, one may refer to his admission, repeated several times in his paper, to the effect that he does not know the African as a people. He says that Africans keep him at arm's length. His inquisitive overtures are always recip-rocated with the now proverbial African smile. It seems to us that this admission should, in fact, have completed the paper. Was there a compulsion to continue in spite of this knowledge? The writer admits to an unusual amount of unrest over this problem ('*Hierdie twyfel maak mens onrustig*').[1] There is an explicit admission of being an 'outsider' in that situation. One may only assume that he continued to contemplate this problem because of some intellectual discomfort. What may be considered the most important ideas arising from his reflections?

In addition to the themes covered in the summary, the following points are, inter alia, raised in the paper: It is reported

---

[1] 'This doubt makes people feel uneasy.'

that the African negates his identity and strives for equality and sameness with the white man. The African, we are told, is concrete; he lives with the 'things'. He is not abstract like his white counterpart. It is argued that in the rural (semi-rural) setting of the University of the North there is peace and calm and the African people appear to be in harmony with their land-scape. In order to capture the meaning of time for the African, the author gives a detailed description of how African workers at the university go about their daily work. He is decent enough not to suggest, as others have done, that these workers by taking their time over a piece of work were simply being lazy. The author arrives at the conclusion that Africans live in the past and in the present, not in terms of an anticipated future. They live from day to day, he says.

I would like to spend a little more time on those workers. It is reported that they were working at a snail's pace; they were talking about women, about trivialities, about the past. It did not matter to them when they finished the job; they even sang some uninspiring tunes. As usual, this tempo was tempo-rarily disrupted by the appearance of the white supervisor (white time). Things changed. The men worked faster. They suddenly had a notion of the future, an idea that the work had to be completed. As soon as the white supervisor had made his retreat, they are reported to have regressed into black time. The writer's only explanation for this absurd story is that African time is slow – 'slower than that of the white'. Could this be an adequate explanation? Decidedly not. I have tried to offer some explanations elsewhere in this book.

Here I would only like to make the following additional observations: It seems to me that if the writer had not been so compelled to prove a point he probably would have remembered a few ideas about motivation, particularly the complexities of work motivation. He would have been forced to arrive at different types of conclusions. I would like him for a moment to imagine himself outside his observation point (his office) as one of those workers. He works a full day at starvation wages. Let us say he has eight children and let us add four wives to that crowd. Let us also say that he is only allowed to work in Pietersburg and its environs. Let him ask himself whether he would have plans about the future. Let him ask himself whether he would care about when the job would get done. Let him also know that the mere presence of the supervisor means that he might lose his job. He should know all that because that is the existential experience of all those workers. If he experienced all that, he would know that the conclusion about fast time and slow time tends to beg the question.

I suggested earlier that Prof. Engelbrecht had strayed too far afield. In his paper, he also presents the case of a patient he 'examined' at Pietersburg Hospital. According to his report, this was an African man who had presented at the hospital complaining of palpitations, pain in his chest, fatigue and weakness of his lower limbs. Neurological and other examinations could not demonstrate active organic pathology. It is reported that this man found himself estranged from his body and his environment. He felt and believed that all other people were against him and that objects in the street appeared to be moving too fast. It is also reported that this man had worked for a merchant as a messenger, using a bicycle for his errands. Before his admission to hospital, the outfitter's shop at which he was employed had been bought over by an energetic young man. It is suggested that this resulted in a change in the tempo of work at the shop. The author arrives at the conclusion that this patient was a neurotic man whose condition must have been associated with the change in the time tempo (the introduction of white time).

I did not examine the patient. That much I must admit. I do have a sneaking feeling that Prof. Engelbrecht was dealing with a self-fulfilling prophecy. He appears to have expected to find a disturbance related to the time dimension at the core of that neurosis. Indeed that is what he found! Even experienced clinicians do find themselves in that kind of situation now and again. Had he been a trained clinician he would have found it extremely difficult to unearth the mechanism which was involved in that man's neurosis. In fact, I doubt whether he asked the right sort of questions, which would have had a greater probability of leading him to more meaningful conclusions. That man's new employer may have been a slave-driver in more than one sense, in more than the sense of an increased tempo of time. He may have been dictatorial; he may have abused and insulted the dignity of that man. He may have had nothing to do with it all. Prof. Engelbrecht should never hope to know all that. The smile will always be there to obscure the existential realities – to take care of business – to obscure the sources of the neuroses.

I leave aside the problem of the future since reference has already been made to it in 'Us and Them'. What requires analysis is the writer's understanding of the black man's frustration and aggression. It is his experience that Africans are frustrated. He observes that the African has a natural aggressive reaction (whatever that means). Reference is also made to the fact that there has been a development of a Black Power movement since 1967. His understanding is that this is not directed against white South Africa but is merely a symptom of the black man's frustration. So far so good. What follows is probably the most interesting social diagnosis of the year. He writes:

Dieperliggend egter is 'n gevoel van frustrasie, 'n soek na die 'eie ek' wat verlore en opgebreek word. Die swart gebalde vuis is nie slegs 'n teken van swartmag en swart-bewussyn nie, maar veel eeder [sic] 'n symbool van aggressie – van botsing in sigself en tussen drome en werklikheid. Die swart vuis is nie soseer gemik teen die witman en sy wêreld nie, maar teen die swart man en sy frustrasies self – teen sy andersheid d.w.s. teen die gelykmakers. Dit is eerder 'n hand wat gryp in 'n leegt [sic] – na niks.[2] (Engelbrecht, 1972: 27)

I have quoted Engelbrecht verbatim so that I cannot be accused of having misrepresented him. He is convinced that the black man's frustration is a result of lost identity and a search for that identity. The black clenched fist should, according to him, be understood as having very little to do with Black Power or Black Consciousness. It should be understood as being directed at the black himself with his frustrations. The fist is directed also at those people who say that we are all the same. The fist, we are told with contempt, is a hand which is grasping at nothing. The professor maintains that the people who say that we are all the same create frustrations in the black man and make him dream! Even the most *verkrampte* Afrikaner will admit in private gossip that there are many other reasons for the black man's frustrations which are far removed from the issue of an identity crisis.[3] Pap, hostels, removals, pass laws, being beaten up on the highways.

---

[2] 'Beneath there is a sense of frustration, a search for the self that gets lost and fragmented. The black clenched fist is not only a sign of Black Power and Black Consciousness, but much rather a symbol of aggression – of conflict within and between dream and reality. The black fist is not so much aimed at the white man and his world as against the black man and his own frustrations – against his otherness, and that is against those that want to make him the same. Rather, it is a hand grabbing air, not just nothingness.'

[3] *Verkrampte* is an Afrikaans term that refers to a conservative or reactionary person of Afrikaner origin.

It is interesting to note that Prof. Engelbrecht announces
a lack of interest in matters political. In spite of this bold and
unexpected posture, we find him wallowing in the politics of
separate development. As if that were not enough, he tails off his
paper by giving an air of respectability to his claims by quoting
Prof. J.H. van den Berg out of context:[4]

*Psychoterapeut zijn onze dagen: het betekent advocaat zijn
van rechtvaardige ongelijkheid.*[5]

---

[4] J.H. van den Berg (1914–2012) was a Dutch psychiatrist who adopted a
phenomenological approach and was interested in the psychology of historical change. His text *The Changing Nature of Man* (1956) was highly influential
amongst liberal and critically oriented psychologists in South Africa. Van den
Berg, who visited South Africa, was concerned to show how historical circumstances influenced the presentation of psychopathology and would have been
critical of the 'timeless nonsense' propounded by Engelbrecht that Manganyi
criticises.

[5] 'To be a psychotherapist in our day *means to legitimate being different.*' This
clarifies why Manganyi wishes to point out how out of context Engelbrecht's
usage of Van den Berg is. To fully demonstrate the context of this sentence,
and hence Engelbrecht's inappropriate usage, here is the paragraph
where it appears in Van den Berg (1956, emphasis in original).

*De psychotherapeut laat de patiënt zijn eigen, onvervreemdbare ongelijkheid
vinden. Psychotherapeut zijn in onze dagen: het betekent advocaat zijn
van rechtvaardige ongelijkheid. Of anders uitgedrukt: psychotherapeut
zijn bestaat erin fenomenologisch op die onderscheidingen te wijzen, waarin
'anderszijn' tot zijn recht komt en waarin* uniciteit *ernstig wordt genomen.*

The psychotherapist allows the patient to find his/her own inalien-
able difference. To be a psychotherapist in our day *means to legitimate
being different.* Or, to put it differently: To be a psychotherapist means
to phenomenologically highlight those differences in which 'to be
different' comes into its own, and in which *uniqueness* is being taken
seriously.

I insist this tailpiece is out of context because I am also familiar with Prof. van den Berg's views on the matter of equality and sameness. His fundamental thesis appears to be that one who is sane may not legitimately say that Bach or Mozart is equal to the man who drives a train to Soweto. This is legitimate. There appear to be no reasonable grounds for extending this idea from the area of psychotherapy to broad sociological planning.

Park Station, Johannesburg, in the morning, in the evening, during the day – a mad rushing about of black people in all directions. Black time? White time? The question is absurd. It is my contention that Prof. Engelbrecht generalises so frivolously because he is politically motivated; motivated by a compulsive desire to defend separate development.

References

Beneš, V. (1968) *Spinal Cord Injury*. London: Baillière, Tindall & Cassel.

Benton, A.L. (1959) *Right-left Discrimination and Finger Localization: Development and Pathology*. New York: Harper and Harper.

Buber, M. (1958) *I and Thou*. 2nd edn. Translated by R.G. Smith. Edinburgh: T. & T. Clark.

Bugental, J.F.T. (1967) *Challenges of Humanistic Psychology*. New York: McGraw-Hill.

Camus, A. (1955) *The Myth of Sisyphus*. London: Hamish Hamilton.

Caplan, G. (1970) *The Theory and Practice of Mental Health Consultation*. New York: Basic Books.

Carothers, J.C. (1953) *The African Mind in Health and Disease*. Geneva: WHO.

Democracy Now (2013) *Polaroid & Apartheid: Inside the Beginnings of the Boycott, Divestment Movement Against South Africa*. 13 December. https://www.democracynow.org/2013/12/13/polaroid_apartheid_inside_the_beginnings_of (accessed 10 June 2019).

De Ridder, J.C. (1961) *The Personality of the Urban African in South Africa: A Thematic Apperception Test Study*. London: Routledge & Kegan Paul.

Engelbrecht, F.J. (1972) 'Tyd en Neurose by die Bantoe'. Pietersburg: Universiteit van die Noorde. Publikasies van die Universiteit van die Noorde; Reeks A, No. 16.

Fisher, S. and Cleveland, S.E. (1968a) 'Reappraisal: A Review of Developments from 1958–1967', in Fisher, S. and Cleveland, S.E. *Body Image and Personality*. 2nd rvd edn. Princeton, N.J.: Van Nostrand.

Fisher, S. and Cleveland, S.E. (1968b) *Body Image and Personality*. 2nd rvd edn. Princeton, N.J.: Van Nostrand.

Frankl, V.E. (1965) *The Doctor and the Soul: From Psychotherapy to Logotherapy*. 2nd expanded edn. New York: Alfred A. Knopf.

Frankl, V.E. (1967) *Psychotherapy and Existentialism: Selected Papers on Logotherapy*. New York: Simon & Schuster.

Fromm, E. (1941) *Escape from Freedom*. Oxford: Farrar & Rinehart.

Gertsmann, J. (1958) 'Psychological and Phenomenological Aspects of Disorders of the Body Image', *Journal of Nervous and Mental Diseases*, 126, pp. 449–512.

Grobbelaar, A. (1972) 'Getting Rid of Labour Anarchy', *Rand Daily Mail*, 2 November, p. 14.

Gutkind, P.C.W. (ed.) (1970) *The Passing of Tribal Man in Africa*. Leiden: E.J. Brill.

Hellman, E. (1971) *Soweto*. Johannesburg: South African Institute of Race Relations.

Holleman, J.F. *et al.* (eds.) (1964) *Problems of Transition*. Pietermaritzburg: Natal University Press.

Khoapa, B. (1972) 'The New Black', in Biko, S. (ed.) *Black Viewpoint*. Durban: Spro-Cas Black Community Programmes, pp. 61–67.

Kolb, L.C. (1959) 'Disturbances of the Body Image', in Arieti, S. (ed.) *American Handbook of Psychiatry*, Vol. 1. New York: Basic Books, pp. 749–769.

Kouwer, B.J. (1953) 'Gelaat en Karacter', in Van den Berg, J.H. en Linkschoten, J. (rds.) *Persoon en Wêreld: Bijdragen tot de Phaenomenologische Psychologie*. Utrecht: Erven J. Bijleveld, pp. 59–73.

Langner, T.S. and Michael, S.T. (1963) *Life Stress and Mental Health: II. The Midtown Manhattan Study*. Oxford, England: Free Press Glencoe.

Leighton, D.C. and Leighton, A.H. (1967) 'Mental Health and Social Factors', in Freedman, A.M. and Kaplan, H.A. (eds.) *Comprehensive Textbook of Psychiatry*. Oxford, England: Williams and Wilkins, pp. 1520–1533.

LeVine, R.A. (1970) 'Personality and Change', in Paden, J.N. and Soja, E.W. (eds.) *The African Experience*, Vol. 1. London: Heinemann Educational Books, pp. 276–303.

Lifton, R.J. (1961) *Thought Reform and the Psychology of Totalism: A Study of 'Brainwashing' in China*. New York: W.W. Norton.

Manganyi, N.C. (1972a) 'Body Image Boundary Differentiation and Self-steering Behaviour in African Paraplegics', *Journal of Personality Assessment*, 36 (1), pp. 45–49.

Manganyi, N.C. (1972b) 'Psychotherapy and Psycho-social Relativity', *Journal of Behavioural Science*, 1 (4), pp. 189–192.

May, R. (1967) *Psychology and the Human Dilemma*. New York: Van Nostrand.

Mayer, P. (1961) *Townsmen or Tribesmen: Conservatism and the Process of Urbanization in a South African City*. Contributions by I Mayer. Cape Town: Oxford University Press. Series: Xhosa in Town, Studies of the Bantu-speaking Population of East London, Cape Province; No. 2.

Mayer, P. (1972) *Urban Africans and the Bantustans*. The Alfred and Winifred Hoernlé Memorial Lecture. Johannesburg: South African Institute of Race Relations.

Merleau-Ponty, M. (1962) *Phenomenology of Perception*. London: Routledge & Kegan Paul.

Moolman, J.H. (1971) 'Urbanisation of the Bantu in South Africa', USSALEP (United States – South Africa Leadership Development Programme) Symposium. Johannesburg.

Moolman, J.H. (1972) 'Peaceful Coexistence in the Spatial System of the R.S.A.', *Bulletin of the Africa Institute of South Africa*, X (10), pp. 416–419.

Nel, B.F. (1967) *Antropologiese Aanloop tot 'n Verantwoordelike Psigologiese Pedagogiek*. Stellenbosch: Universiteits Uitgewers.

Niebuhr, R. (1966) *Man's Nature and His Communities*. London: Geoffrey Bles.

Paden, J.N. and Soja, E.W. (eds.) (1970) *The African Experience*, Vol. l. London: Heinemann Educational Books.

Pauw, B.A. (1963) *The Second Generation: A Study of the Family among Urbanized Bantu in East London*. Cape Town: Oxford University Press. Series: Xhosa in Town, Studies of the Bantu-speaking Population of East London, Cape Province; No. 3.

Randall, P. (ed.) (1971) *Towards Social Change*. Spro-Cas Publication Number 6. Report of the Social Commission of the Study Project on Christianity in Apartheid Society. Johannesburg: Spro-Cas.

Randall, P. (ed.) (1972) *Power, Privilege and Poverty*. Spro-Cas Publication Number 7. Report of the Economics Commission of the Study Project on Christianity in Apartheid Society. Johannesburg: Spro-Cas.

Reader, D.H. (1961) *The Black Man's Portion: History, Demography, and Living Conditions in the Native Locations of East London,*

Cape Province. Cape Town: Oxford University Press. Series: Xhosa in Town, Studies of the Bantu-speaking Population of East London, Cape Province; No. 1.

Sartre, J.-P. (1949) *Nausea*. Translated by L. Alexander. Norfolk, CT: New Directions.

Sartre, J.-P. (1956) *Being and Nothingness: An Essay on Phenomenological Ontology*. Translated by H.E. Barnes. New York: Philosophical Library.

Schilder, P. (1964) *Contributions to Developmental Neuropsychiatry*. New York: International Universities Press.

Schlemmer, L. (1971) 'Strategies for Change', in Randall, P. (ed.) *Towards Social Change*. Spro-Cas Publication Number 6. Report of the Social Commission of the Study Project on Christianity in Apartheid Society. Johannesburg: Spro-Cas, pp. 156–192.

Senghor, L.S. (1966) 'Négritude: A Humanism of the 20th Century', *Optima*, 16 (1), pp. 1–8.

Shontz, F.C. (1969) *Perceptual and Cognitive Aspects of Body Experience*. New York: Academic Press.

Silberbauer, E.R. (1968) *Understanding and Motivating the Bantu Worker*. Johannesburg: Personnel Management Advisory Service.

Sorokin, P.A. (1941) *The Crisis of Our Age*. New York: E.P. Dutton.

South African History Online. (2014) *1973 Durban Strikes. Introduction*. https://www.sahistory.org.za/article/1973-durban-strikes (accessed 29 April 2019).

Sternbach, R.A. (1968) *Pain: A Psychophysiological Analysis*. New York: Academic Press.

Tempels, P. (1959) *Bantu Philosophy*. Translated by C. King. Paris: Présence Africaine.

Tobias, P.V. (1972) *The Meaning of Race*. 2nd edn. Johannesburg: South African Institute of Race Relations.

Van den Berg, J.H. (1953) 'Verantwoording', in Van den Berg, J.H. en Linkschoten, J. (rds.) *Persoon en Wêreld: Bijdragen tot de Phaenomenologische Psychologie.* Utrecht: Erven J. Bijleveld, pp. 1–10.

Van den Berg, J.H. (1956) *Metabletica: Beginselen van Een Historische Psychologie* [*The Changing Nature of Man: Introduction to a Historical Psychology*]. Nijkerk: Callenbach.

Van den Berg, J.H. (1964) *De Psychiatrische Patient.* Nijkerk: G.F. Gallenbach N.V.

Van den Berg, J.H. (1966) *The Psychology of the Sickbed.* Pittsburgh, P.A.: Duquesne University Press.

Van den Berg, J.H. (1971) 'What Is Psychotherapy?', *Humanitas, Journal of the Institute of Man,* VII (3), pp. 321–370.

Wilson, M. (1964) 'The Coherence of Groups', in Holleman, J.F. *et al.* (eds.) *Problems of Transition.* Pietermaritzburg: Natal University Press, pp. 1–20.

Witkin, H.A. *et al.* (1962) *Psychological Differentiation: Studies of Development.* New York: Wiley.

Glossary

African personality: see Négritude.

Anthropology: In the sense of the study of man in his wholeness.

Anxiety state: A neurotic disorder whose main feature is the existence of unaccountable pervasive anxiety.

Body boundary: A theoretical construct in body image studies meant to account for definiteness or indefiniteness of the body's exterior.

Body image: A mental representation of one's body.

Counselling: A fairly inclusive term for a variety of ways of helping individuals in difficulty achieve better adaptation.

Dialogue: In the sense of relating.

Dimensional ontology: Frankl's belief that being human means being body, psyche and 'spirit'.

Eschatology: The science of death, judgement, heaven and hell (theological).

Existentialism: A twentieth-century European philosophical and literary movement whose concerns are those of man in the world.

Hypothesis: A scientific hunch for experimental verification.

Ideological totalism: Complete unquestioning commitment to an ideology.

Mental health consultation: A service in community mental health provided by mental health specialists to clients.

Négritude: The totality of the cultural values of the black world, the black lifestyle.

Noetic: Of the spirit, as used by Frankl.

Ontology: The analysis of being and existence.

Phantom limb: Ghost limb; a feeling that an amputated limb is still in existence and functional.

Positivism: A position which holds that knowledge is limited to observable facts and experience.

Psychotherapy: The use of specialised methods in the treatment of mental disorders.

Schizophrenia: A psychotic reaction accompanied by marked personality disorganisation.

Transcendentalism: In philosophy, a system which is characterised by idealism and visionary qualities.

Vital force: A spirit which has force in African ontology.

Afterword

'Being-Black-in-the-World' and the Future of 'Blackness'
Njabulo S. Ndebele

I

The #RhodesMustFall movement began at the University of Cape Town (UCT) on 9 March 2015. On that day human faeces were thrown at the commemorative statue of Cecil John Rhodes. Until then, the statue of the controversial entrepreneur and benefactor who donated land on which the university was built had dominated the commemorative heraldry of the university. With an imperial loftiness Rhodes pondered the world spread out in front of him, as well as that he presumed existed behind him. He would do that in perpetuity. To this new breed of student the statue's daily dominance and the history it recalled, despite his philanthropy, had become intolerable. The defacement of the statue was soon followed by calls for it to be removed. A debate ensued nationally about history and commemorative statues, but it did not save Rhodes's statue. On 9 April 2015, one month after the student movement had begun, the statue was swiftly and dramatically removed.

Student protesters deemed the statue a painful relic of colonial times; except that this relic, they argued, continued to breathe life into the economic order and the social arrangements supported by it on campus and in the larger society beyond. Its imperial effects have displayed a resilience often glaring but sometimes not easy to recognise in the post-apartheid present. The removal of the Rhodes statue would also serve as the onset of the 'decolonisation' of UCT, a process in which the adverse effects of a colonial legacy could be unveiled, altered or replaced by a new order. The demands of the student movement subsequently spread to other campuses in South Africa, their disruptive intent acquiring a global reach. They were to resonate also at Oxford University where Rhodes exerts a significant commemorative presence.

At the heart of the call for the 'decolonisation' of UCT was a more elemental source of student disaffection: being 'black' in a 'white' world. The #RhodesMustFall movement projected 'blackness' as a critical element in the discourse of protest against the 'whiteness' of Rhodes's legacy and its resilient effects. The 'black body in pain' needed to be affirmed as human against its dehumanising depreciation as exploited labour in more than a century of captured service to Rhodes's imperial, capitalist vision and the strong racist character that drove it. The colonial economic system and its politics established, developed and embedded superior–inferior relationships between 'white' and 'black' humans respectively. It is common to approach this relationship from the perspective of its driving agency: 'whites' oppressing 'blacks', or civilised 'whites' as superior humans oppressing uncivilised, sub-human 'blacks'. In reality, the system dehumanised both. It is the less recognised dehumanisation of 'whites' by the very system they created which is the target of the uncovering intent of the 'decolonial' project.

It is to be assumed that part of the 'decolonial' project is to change the attitudes of 'whites' towards 'blacks' by getting them to abandon racist attitudes and behaviour associated with them as a group. The urgency in this has to do with the perception that South African 'whites' did not give up much to make the post-apartheid reconciliation project more successful. 'Whites' seemed to assume that the country they claim to have 'built' would in 1994 and beyond remain as desirable to everyone else as it was to them, regardless of the fact that millions of 'blacks' had been on the inhumane receiving end of its being 'built'.

So what is expected of 'white' South Africans, unveiled as equally dehumanised by their own hand, in a new constitutional democracy? Should they display guilt and remorse? Should they now identify themselves as African: wear African clothes and eat African cuisine? Should they learn to speak African languages and adopt African names, and African cultures of respect and civility? Should they become a part of the popular 'black' sporting preferences and support Bafana Bafana as the national soccer team? Should they explore the prospect of some of them moving from 'white' suburbs to the 'townships'? What about the extraordinary wealth they collectively accumulated on questionable historical, moral and ethical grounds? Will they go about sharing it, while transferring some of the skills employed in acquiring it without the cultures of oppression that removed fair competition between South African citizens? The list of the forms of behavioural transformation expected of them is potentially infinite, but it could be reduced to a single item.

It is reasonable to expect that 'white' South Africans disentangle themselves from a pre-1994 social order in which injustice and unfairness had been institutionalised. The impact of such an order on personal and group conduct, towards themselves and others outside of the group, was so deep that it takes a purposeful unlearning for them to change and then to open themselves to new learning with others. It was clear by 1994 that South Africa, despite its best official ideological intentions up to that point, was by struggle and default evolving into a different society. Public and private institutions would have to radically review what Dinika Govender in an open letter to talk show host John Robbie called their 'cultural architecture'.

Perhaps the question of what is to be expected of 'white' South Africans can partly be answered by asking another one: What did the 'blacks' of South Africa have to do once they had been conquered? There is a long list here. Among others they had to give up their social and economic systems as they had lived these for generations before the arrival of 'whites'; they were forced to become workers; they dispersed over the entire southern African landscape to work; in their travels and places of work they experienced new geographies, exchanged languages and cultural practices. Over time they intermarried on a massive scale, further blurring ethnic and cultural boundaries and rendering them more and more porous; they became cosmopolitan Southern Africans in ways that 'whites' who had consigned them to servitude, and locked in their legalised privileges, were unable to. Working in 'white' people's homes, they got to know far more about 'whites' than 'whites' bothered to learn about them; and as the economy grew in its requirements beyond the control of those who had 'built' it, 'blacks', in addition to being workers, became graduates, managers, lawyers, scientists, engineers, politicians, chief executive officers and state presidents. Over 150 years, they evolved into a different people.

The question of who becomes what or who after being something they would rather not continue to be can be simplistic and complex all at once. Descriptions can typify simplistically at the same time as they can amplify in meaningful, complex ways. The question suggests that for South Africans, compelled by a set of historical circumstances to cooperate, at first, out of a system of structured compulsions, later the energies released out of such compulsions become too powerful to be contained by compulsion. They now have to enter the space of dynamic interactions across race. Interethnic interactions as a result of compelled congregation in places of work and residence have been happening all along.[1] By definition that space will now be coloured by the numerical primacy of those once disenfranchised. Thus, by another definition, the responsibility of the now enfranchised to play the leadership role that their numbers demand, is enormous in a mandatory kind of way. What is the society the once conquered, disenfranchised and newly enfranchised envision for all?

Against the reality of the unfolding of the student protest movement, a question began to emerge for me: If 'black pain' was a state of being to which those who were 'black' felt consigned, not only in the respective institutions in which they found themselves but in the general societal environment, what is it that constituted relief from 'black pain'? It seemed to me that this was a deeply historical question whose import resonated beyond the political moment. There had to be a notion of

---

[1] This happened despite official attempts to divide populations of urban townships for the oppressed into ethnic entities.

'black' well-being and objective conditions that supported it, for it to be affirmed and in which it could flourish. What were the features of the alternative identity and social value of 'black' well-being after the termination of 'black pain' when 'whiteness' had been removed from the scene? What *is* 'black' well-being? In what kind of society would it flourish? Would there still be 'blackness' after the demise of 'whiteness'?

I began to ponder these questions in a brief discussion paper entitled 'The End of Blackness?' presented at the Effects of Race group seminar at the Stellenbosch Institute for Advanced Study in July 2015. It is not a title I chose without some trepidation. For a start, I felt that a paper with such a title, presented as it was at that very moment that the #RhodesMustFall movement arose at the University of Stellenbosch, could be seen as provocative and controversial. As it turned out, three of the student leaders of the movement at that university were present at the seminar and participated in the discussion. It turned out to be a discussion worth having.

Indeed, as the movement unfolded across the country, the seminar was my first opportunity to confront in a space of collective thought what was beginning to gel in my mind. It seemed to me that a great deal of what I heard from the movement came across as very similar to what I and my generation said some forty years ago. I sensed a vital connection with the energy at play. What seemed new to the current generation of students came across to me as a replay of times past under different circumstances. A thought then crystallised: I faced an intergenerational dissonance. What were the dynamics of such dissonance? What did it all mean?

For a start I could attempt a comparative perspective. If 'black pain' is a current reality on our historically 'white' campuses, forty years ago my 'black pain' was far less campus-based than it was a result of a more generalised sense of being oppressed across the entire South African landscape. The apartheid-imposed limitations on my movements were remarkably countered by an internal sense of expansiveness I experienced as the very meaning of Black Consciousness at the time. A being externally depreciated in value by an exploitative economic order discovered profound inner value. My fear of 'white' people, no matter how economically or militarily powerful they may have been, was replaced by an enormous sense of inner possibility and power which did not in any way minimise the brutal reality of what could happen to me were I to fall into the hands of the 'white' system. Despite the overt power of the racially oppressive system, there was something in me beyond its reach. Something in the national environment, articulated on some individual campuses in 2015, had reached the inner core of 'black' students and appeared to have destabilised that core significantly. What was it in the two decades of democracy that led to this situation?

There was another historical reality. The majority of 'black' students in South African higher education forty years ago were registered in 'historically black universities'. They were on campus as a manifestation of what 'black' people had to do if they wanted a university education. They were required to apply to institutions specifically designated for them. There, they were 'blacks' first and 'black students' after. There, their colour was a given and required little justification. There was something numerically normal about that situation. 'Black' people were just too many to exterminate, and their labour too vital for such extermination to be contemplated. The 'white' state needed to devise ways to control them in their vast numbers. In the total scheme of things it was impossible for the 'white' South African state to close the doors of human aspiration for people to participate in the fullest complexity of social endeavour even if 'white' ideology demanded otherwise. Thus in the context in which Black Consciousness evolved, 'black' students were naturally more vocal where the stakes for their being 'black' were considerably higher. They were the voice of a downtrodden people.

From the beginning 'black' presence on a 'white' campus has had to be justified. A legal instrument was created to administer and process such justification. An argument had to be and still has to be advanced for 'black' students to be there, even after two decades of democracy. Thus, 'black' students on a 'white' campus carry a sense of self-awareness, of 'intruding', with which their fellow students at 'black' campuses are not burdened. But the latter carry a different burden: the burden of class and the perception of institutional inferiority. Yet 'black' students at 'historically black universities' are comparatively less vocal as 'blacks' than those at 'historically white institutions'. Numerical size and 'cultural architecture' seem to modulate self-awareness, self-acceptance and identity.

Forty years later, in a country that has been in 'black' hands for twenty-three years, I feel far more in a 'black' country than in a 'white' one. In this 'black' country, I feel no insistent compulsion to be designated 'black', much less to designate myself as such. Then staring at me is a dissonance of the moment: that between a current generation of 'black' students who treasure the designation 'black' and an older generation that is less insistent on the designation. Between the older generation and the overwhelmingly vast majority of 'black' students on 'black' campuses is the question: What is the prospect for less stridency on 'black' identity and greater confidence in engaging with historic opportunity in an environment that is 'black' in a state of its own being and without the requirement of definition? But the relative minority of 'black' students at 'white' institutions seem uniquely placed in a space to sharpen the critique of that historic opportunity. One can see in this the prospect of a student movement across the higher education system that is founded on an entirely different set of activist premises. What could be the enabling historical context for such premises?

II

In 1973 Chabani Manganyi published the book *Being-Black-in-the-World*. Reading this book in 2016 led me to ask another set of questions. What if #RhodesMustFall student activists had in large numbers encountered this book in their undergraduate syllabus at any South African university they had chosen to attend? What if they had studied this book together with the writings of Steve Biko and Frantz Fanon and other related books as standard curriculum fare across the various disciplines in a country so remarkably described by James L. Gibson as historically unique in its direct and thorough confrontation of 'its past in an effort to shape its future' (2004: 1)? The story of such confrontation would have been expected to be the preoccupation of a learning country. This does not appear to have been the case.

There are many more books which could have formed the base of a shared, foundational or intellectual culture in the educational system. This could have happened across the body of knowledge spanning fiction, biography, autobiography, poetry, drama, history, political science, philosophy, anthropology, sociology and science. A store of books and other educational media across these fields of knowledge would have become standard fare in a curriculum to stimulate imaginative thinking and speculation about a new society, its contours and its prospects. What would have been the cumulative impact of such knowledge on the #RhodesMustFall discourse on 'blackness' and 'whiteness' in the context in which they were engaged in recent protest? To what extent would the running discourse of protest not only have expressed a broader and deeper awareness of alternative intellectual currents, but also represented a significant advance in a local tradition of radical critique in South Africa?

Of course, individual #RhodesMustFall activists may indeed have been exposed to these thinkers and others. Their exposure to such thinkers is surely the gift of their resourceful, questing spirits, reminiscent of many Black Consciousness activists of the South African Students' Organisation (SASO) in the late 1960s and early 1970s who discovered, on their own, vistas of knowledge that radically expanded their thinking despite prohibitions on, and restrictions to, knowledge by the apartheid state. While such prohibitions and restrictions were formally lifted in 1994, they seemed to have remained by default as a weakness in systemic commitment to a radical, comprehensive and integrated review of the educational curriculum across the entire education system.

SASO student activists' response to systemic prohibition was to read extensively and learn collectively outside of the restricted prescribed syllabus, thus providing a self-motivated subversive norm of alternative learning. Fortuitously, they were laying foundations for encountering the forbidden terrain in which they re-imagined the identity of the oppressed as one centred in their own making of history. Their venture into this re-imagining could well have provided a pedagogical opening towards the imagining of alternative content for a future system of education. It is reasonable and unsurprising that after two decades of freedom, the #RhodesMustFall activists should expect that the legacy of such a subversive norm would by now be the foundational norm of pedagogy in the new South Africa. For its educational system the new democracy should have been far more preoccupied than it has been with this kind of re-imagining.

What if, when they undertook their disruptive activism in 2015, the students had been learning in a public system of education in which they, and their generational peers, were grounded in an alternative local imaginary that had been enjoying systemic affirmation by the new state for two decades? This could have enabled them to acquire a sense of being-in-the-world that would accord them the ability to interact with knowledge systems around the world with some confidence. Against such a background, what would have been the content and tenor of their disruptive discourse?

It is in answer to this last question that Manganyi's writing acquires particular resonance. What is it in *Being-Black-in-the-World* that the students and their teachers would have been grappling with intellectually? In all likelihood they would have been shaped by a discourse of critique different to that built on the foundations laid in 1994. This situation suggests that in 1994, only one part of the struggle for liberation ended. If that part was the political part, what was the other part, or other parts, that should have begun?

This other part, that is arguably more vital, prompted yet another question: How do South Africans visualise the nature and character of the constitutional society, the fullness of which they have yet to achieve and for which they struggled for close to a century? How did it come about that at the point of liberation the liberated, despite their best intentions, seemed to lose focus? The agenda of transformation seems to stall in the face of a resurgence of the politics of racial conflict reminiscent of pre-1994 conflicts.

III

In *Being-Black-in-the-World* Manganyi conveys a grounded faith in the elemental nature of human transformations that have been going on in Africa before and since the continent's at first curious, and then violent, interaction with Europe. It is here 'on the African continent', he asserts, that 'the great and intricate drama of being black-in-the-world is taking place' (Manganyi, 1973: 3). It is his characterisation of the drama as intricate that captures my attention.

The intricate is necessarily complex. Complexity of any kind can invite impatience and nervousness of the restive or frustrated kind, or it can induce excitement or yearning born of eagerness. The former, in the environment of colonial or apartheid repression, can lead to reactive violence, or to the danger of the 'emotive', while the latter reaction can call the impatient self to order in favour of curiosity and the desires of eagerness to inquire and perhaps to hit on invention and unexpected resourcefulness. Thus, grappling with the intricacies of complexity may indeed result in creativity and inventiveness.

For Manganyi both reactions to complexity, stimulated as they would be by real-life social interactions, call to be understood for what they are. This kind of understanding out of inevitable social engagement is the basis of Manganyi's faith that out of 300 years of a violent, often brutal, interaction between Africa and Europe, a reflective and activist African agency can arise and restore African selfhood and inventive assertiveness in reshaping the human face of the world.

If there are intricacies in the drama of 'being-black-in-the-world', the work of Charles van Onselen (1996) has shown that relationships between 'black' and 'white' South Africans have generated their own set of intricacies. Mutual dependence and interdependence are possible even in inherently conflicted human situations. Intricate relationships arise when unavoidable contact between people generates some logic of cooperation. South Africa has been a space for such logics to play out for three centuries. In 1994 yet another phase began in that kind of history. Without this kind of perspective South Africans may become a record that keeps playing on the same scratch, placing themselves outside of evolutionary renewal.

It is against such a context that Manganyi argues that 'being-in-the-world' with a 'black body' has similar human implications as 'being-in-the-world' with a 'white body'. The fundamental similarity in both experiences of being-in-the-world is in the shared human necessity to make culture, which 'may be understood as constituting the most concrete medium for the structuring of the dialogue between man and the universe' (Manganyi, 1973: 37). If there are any differences, they are differences of lifestyle indicative of different ways in the respective histories of being in dialogue with the world.

Significantly, Manganyi conceives of the relationship between people and their environment as dialogical. What is different between people, as in the same manner that their cuisine may be different, is in the nature of the 'dialogue' each 'being-in-the-world' has with itself, with the people around it and the world of objects around it. The sense of history and of being in it emerges from these three forms of dialogical interaction singly or in combination.

There ought then to be a decisive difference in what 'being-black-in-the-world' is able to deploy in its recovery from what has been a fraught dialogical interaction over several centuries with 'being-white-in-the-world'. More than bringing attention to its pain at the hands of its aggressive, oppressing antagonist, Manganyi seems to be saying, 'being-black-in-the-world' must foreground the values of its lifestyle, a product of its culture-making proclivity which may be fundamentally different and potentially more self-enabling in confronting and negotiating a persistently hostile and dominating 'being-white-in-the-world'. At stake is the human view of the world as oppressed 'blacks' have seen it and lived it, even in the most difficult existential circumstances, and continue to see it and often value it as they re-establish their place in the world.

Thus far, the 'blacks' have yet to project with sufficient confidence, knowledge and authority their perspective of 'being-black-in-the-world'. Against five centuries of 'being-white-in-the-world', dominating the world and the repressive cultures of that dominance, further restrained and contained as it has been by its existential discomfort with the condition of oppression, 'being-black-in-the-world' has yet to deploy the liberatory potential of its world view with authority and decisiveness.

Such self-assertion is critical if the perspective of 'being-white-in-the-world' has to seriously engage with an alternative value system, particularly that resurging, reforming, recreating and emerging from worlds doggedly repressed by 'whiteness'. The urgency of challenging 'being-white-in-the-world' with new self-affirmations by the liberated humanity of 'being-black-in-the-world' takes on greater significance against the background of other changes occurring in the world. The demographic ascendance of the so-called Global South, beyond numerical superiority, taking full advantage of a technological inheritance and aspects of an economic system that once oppressed them, is a case in point. 'Being-white-in-the-world' has to take note and to respond according to a new logic of adaptation against the background of its own increasing loss of dominance.

In the South African context, such a development makes possible the emergence of a new set of relationships that promise over time a kind of functional parity working to benefit a common identity that is forged out of a collaborative mutuality in a constitutional democracy. It becomes decisively critical that the 'black–white' relationship not assume a hegemonic dominance as a public preoccupation, as has been the case up to this point. In this fundamental adjustment in relations between world views, 'blacks' are poised to bring far more onto the stage than their 'pain'. There is more to the world than the history of 'white' racism.

Indeed, the freedom from the colonial and apartheid preoccupation with the 'black–white' relationship ought to promise new worlds. The 'black–black' relationship is no longer what it was at the time of conquest. It has evolved phenomenally through social coagulations in the mines, factories, farms and township settlements. Languages, customs, music, cuisines, dances and world views were exchanged and shared, thus making intra-tribal affiliations less restrictive and more porous and open to other affiliations across the national sphere. Such exchanging and sharing, as alluded to, created widespread interpersonal relationships that resulted in almost universal intermarrying across tribe, geography, religion, education and class, cutting through often received restrictive cultural boundaries.

While this coagulation may have taken place over time and through compulsions of various kinds, it is not easy to dispel the notion that the establishment in January 1912 of the South African Native National Congress (SANNC), which later became the African National Congress, provided formative ideological

129

affirmations which underscored *non-tribalism* as a formative value. It is for this reason that this value of non-tribalism should have stood side by side with non-racialism and non-sexism in section 1, chapter 1, of the founding provisions of the Constitution of the Republic of South Africa. For over a hundred years of struggle this value was durable in its ability to unify 'black' South Africans against the declared objective of the apartheid state to create and consolidate tribal divisions through dogged state intervention. Non-tribalism has been a formative value in the social cohesion of the 'black' oppressed and now offers space to enter for 'white' South Africans detribalised from their 'whiteness'.

The SANNC was the African response to 'the racial exclusion and discrimination under the new Union of South Africa, established in 1910. Cross-tribal from the outset, but limited to the nascent 'black' intelligentsia, it spread its representativeness across class, education, and geographic barriers encompassing the southern African region from which South African capitalism recruited its labour. SANNC aspired to unite Africans in the advancement of their political and socio-economic status'.[2]

This speaks to the issue that without the de-centring of the 'black–white' relation, racial thinking in South Africa might persist to the hegemonic advantage of the 'being-white-in-the-world' world view, even when both 'black' and 'white' South Africa might desire otherwise. This is against the historic fact of the aggression of 'being-white-in-the-world' in the last 500 years of world history, such that even the nature of reactive resistance to that aggression in the South African context often comes across as itself having

---

[2] https://www.sahistory.org.za/dated-event/formation-south-african-native-national-congress

been encapsulated in the very spectacle of aggression even as the liberation movement fought the good fight in the long struggle. That is to say, even the resistance to 'being-white-in-the-world' often reproduces in the actions of the 'black' resisters some of their opponents' values and action in the terms and means of combating them. This will remain so for as long as the alternative world view of 'being-black-in-the-world' is absent from the battle-field. What will it take for the 'blacks' of the world, particularly in South Africa, to project a new sense of 'being-in-the-world' that is galvanised not by the sense of burden but by the freedom of agency and initiative?

IV

In a post-1994 South Africa that had committed to achieving its vision of a new society through fundamental changes in the social realm, particularly through the educational curric-ulum, the #RhodesMustFall activists would almost certainly have read and discussed in the university curriculum another seminal work that is almost certain to have shaped their activist discourse. This work presents a rich supplementary and bold experiential context to Manganyi's theoretical rigour.

Native Nostalgia by Jacob Dlamini, equally rigorous in its exploration of the challenge of social visioning, exploded into the South African public sphere in 2009. In this book, Dlamini asks the question: Could someone who has lived in a South African township during apartheid after a long and, by many measures, difficult life ever be nostalgic for that township life? Was it possible to be nostalgic for life deemed pathological? To the chagrin of many habituated to the terrible conditions of township life as a ready and habitual justification for politics of protest, Dlamini answered in the affirmative.[3] Thus, he began a cross-generational conversation with Manganyi.

'We [South Africans],' writes Manganyi, 'have been telling all and sundry that we are capable of teaching the world something novel about racial harmony and peaceful co-existence in a multi-racial (multi-national?) society. Perhaps it is time for us to turn inward and assess whether our claims are not in excess of our progress' (1973: 6). The challenge of 'teaching the world' for South Africans would have to be based on a lot more than declarations to do so, although such declarations may arise out of various emotional moments of a deep and genuine desire to do so. Such desires can indeed have the potential to be one of the 'ties that bind', but all of South Africa has to work at giving reality to those ties.

For 'black' South Africans, 'teaching the world' may well be entangled with what lessons there are to learn and to share with confidence out of the experience of more than a century of living in regulated townships and population-depleted rural communities. This is despite, and perhaps even because of, asserts clinical psychologist Manganyi, having 'the highest cumulative unfavourable social experiences ... to be found. These are populations at special risk, from a mental health point of view' (1973: 6). Yet they are not devoid of value.

However, this acknowledges the reality of 'native nostalgia' for township settlements with the 'highest cumulative

---

[3] It is most fortuitous that as I am writing this, I am listening to a musical group I had never heard of before. It is called The Soil and the name of the album is *Nostalgic Moments*. The album fuses the urban and the rural with an inventive genius that is definitively 'township' and in its authenticity and self-confidence participates in the universal, which is always reflected in local authenticities.

unfavourable social experiences'. Dlamini deploys qualifications about the extent of such nostalgia. For example, he would say, 'native nostalgia' exists despite apartheid, not because of it. But such qualifications, which reflect the complexity of his own thinking, never outweigh the overwhelming evidence by which Dlamini makes us view the township and its possibilities with new eyes.

The ideological isolation of 'black' townships from 'white' suburbs has also carried an unexpected, if unheralded, blessing: the existential absence of 'whites'. Instead, general 'white' presence, in the form of repressive laws, was abstract. This allowed for 'black' existential cultures to emerge over time that gave township life across the country a universal familiarity among those trapped in them. This made possible living spaces inaccessible and unavailable to 'whites' by their own laws, yet formative of 'black' identity over time through 'black' initiative with lived agonies and ecstasies along the way.

On the other hand, the physical, existential reality of 'whites' – out there in their homes with manicured lawns, swimming pools, and servants' quarters, towns, gated suburbs, parks, city halls, shopping malls, offices and factories – was accessible to 'blacks' as workers on a daily basis. As a result, it could be said, 'whites' have a constrained existential knowledge and experience of the totality of the South African human environment. Their predominant experience of that reality has been to devise laws to contain, from their perspective, the 'other', unknown and unknowable. As in 1994 and beyond, South African 'whites', living inside the cocoon of their own creation, were the least prepared to contribute experientially to the challenge of a new human reality in the country. Much of the totality of the South African human environment is alien to the average 'white' South African. Whatever there was of their predominant contribution was out there in the form of the plethora of apartheid laws and what those laws have conveyed of the economic, political and social attitudes that were the bases for their promulgation. Beyond this, there is a human space in the township that no 'being-white-in-the-world' could easily occupy. That space has been the site of both the pain and joy that make 'black' experience so elementally human. It is this space that fascinates Dlamini.

Dlamini has us reflect on several markers of township culture that characterise the township across the land as a space of culture. Township streets flow continuously with human energy. This street energy is a defining feature of the African city to the north of South Africa in, for example, Accra, Lagos, Bamako, Nairobi, Cairo, Dakar and Kampala. This kind of city ambience is generally in sharp contrast to the silent street cultures of South Africa's 'white' suburbs where neighbours may live side by side for many years and exchange greetings mainly on casual mutual sightings. Driving or walking through these suburbs evokes in me to this day the sense of being watched and of the possibility of a police vehicle appearing at any moment for its stern, uniformed occupants to confront me to show why I should not be bundled into the vehicle to cleanse the suburb of me.

To this day, all South African towns and cities die at night. This is not so in the metropolitan cities of the world. There might be a story in there of how 'whiteness' in South Africa perceived its urban communities as spaces of clinical isolation and its postured silences as evidence of the civilised European outpost. I explored a version of this perspective in my essay on South African game parks (Ndebele, 2007). But the differences in city ambience are not necessarily a judgement but a view on lifestyle. Except that in the South African context difference will more often shift beyond the descriptive to the comparative superior–inferior relationship.

One can extrapolate something else from the phenomenon of streets flowing with energy. African cities like most others in the world retain much of their critical mass of human energy that is expended in the spatial setting of home and work. In South Africa, township energy is exported massively to the 'white' urban spatial settings on a daily basis. Thus, the best of township human energy is expended away from its spatial communal life. Townships were designed not to provide for a range of basic human needs: food, clothing and entertainment, and, increasingly, basic education. They were designed not to support Manganyi's dialogical relationship of creativity between people, the communities and their physical world. They were designed to violate that relationship. In townships people were daily forced to enter a dialogical world of 'being-white-in-the-world' in which they would be objects in the hands of a population of those privileged to have legislated away the competition of those they turned into workers. Thus one of the greatest gifts of being human – to work for your own sustenance – was transformed into working for the sustenance of others. It was a dispiriting and dehumanising existence in the oppressive service of others.

Such observations are not made in order to repeat the habitual indictment of 'being-white-in-the world', but rather, and more importantly, to underscore the necessity to re-imagine township environments in which the inhabitants in them grow and flourish from their own energies and that when they go out of the township they carry the sense of who they are from what they have created. It is the act of creating and the conditions in which that creativity takes place that present themselves as decisive in the necessity to effect a radical change in relations of power in which townships, which are home to millions of the South African population, become the centre of gravity in the future human environment of South Africa. In this universe, 'white' suburbs as we see them today would structurally and experientially be ancillary to the greater human transformation in the townships, and no longer the central driver of transformative creative energy in the country.

For the sake of emphasis, Dlamini reflects on one factor, among others, of township life that speaks to the dialogical relationship between inhabitants of the township and their surrounding environment. 'For me,' Dlamini writes,

as I am sure for many of my friends, after-school play was the most important part of our street life. Here we played soccer, marbles, spinning tops, a cricket-like game called *bhathi*, a card game called boom, *umgusha* (high jumps), kites, wire cars and, of course, black *mampatile* (hide-and-seek). But these were not just street games. They heralded in their own way the change in seasons. You could tell what season it was by watching which games children played. Local merchants would know what toys to stock by observing the sequence of games. This was not, however, a simple case of supply and demand but an illustration of a cosmology in which each segment played its part without having to be told what to do. There was, of course, a simple logic to this. Black *mampatile* was a winter game because the sun set early in winter, making it easy to find hiding spots in the dark where boys and girls could make out. There

might also be a far more profound cosmology in the
games children played. (2009: 58–59)

The essence of Dlamini's observations is that first, the social situation he describes played out in exactly the same way in every township. Second, it is remarkable that such distributed practices never achieved organised institutional status in community settings to become an organised skill-based feature of competitive gaming with an established and rooted institutional presence. The weight and extent of restriction on township residents was not only in physical movement, but also by default in the range of imaginative play in social organisation through self-governing institutional architecture created over time out of community practice.

When Africans were conquered, dispossessed and dispersed across the subcontinent, who and what did they become? About the 'what', mostly we can say they became workers. The trajectory of what they became began some 150 years ago and led them all the way to Marikana on 16 August 2012 where the South African Police Service shot protesting workers, killing 34 and wounding 78 of them.[4] What does 'being-white-in-the-world' on behalf of capital do when workers who make 'unreasonable' demands do not return to work, and thus adversely affect the production of platinum that could force the mine out of business? Arrest them. Lay them off. Shoot them. The analogy with captured slaves is not far from the mind. The analogy has been relevant for over a century. It has to give way.

---

[4] https://en.m.wikipedia.org/wiki/Marikana_killings

V

But who Africans became is another trajectory. Who did they become in their overwhelming numbers in townships? Even in the rural areas, those who were not required as labourers and were left there by relatives who went to the distant mines: Who did they become over time? Despite being 'populations at special risk' having 'the highest cumulative unfavourable social experiences . . . to be found' they were, where they were, not slaves. They had the space, no matter how minimal, to create a life. It is this that also fascinates Dlamini. This situation does provide a window to be prised open by a determined, visionary state.

To drive the point home, there is another text that ponders the possibility of this window opening out even further. The title of Ferial Haffajee's new book is in the form of a question: *What If There Were No Whites in South Africa?* With its provocative, tongue-in-cheek title, this book wants to catch the eye of a South African anxious about the future in the present dominated by the past. It approximates the essence of the thought behind the title of my presentation 'The End of Blackness?' It is in restating that the future of South Africa ultimately does not lie in the relationship between 'blacks' and 'whites', but in what happens in the townships and rural areas where the vast majority of South Africans live, and who, when they have created a new world for themselves and all who live in the country, will no longer be 'black' but citizens of South Africa.

Haffajee is disturbed by a rhetoric of protest that calls for changes that are actually occurring such that whatever change has occurred is not seen as part of a list of achievements of the new democracy. The perception of an almost uncontested dominance of 'white' power gives little credit to transformational shifts since 1994. Looking at the world around her, Haffajee avers:

> My life is defined by and led by black power in all its manifestations and tributaries. From where I sit, blacks are the centre of my gaze in all ways.
>
> And this is why I find our narrative of black disempowerment by whites, of black domination by whites, of black marginalisation by whites, so hard to fathom it makes me feel like I am going stark raving mad. I feel as if I've come up against the power that does not know its name or its influence – it is why I think we need a new Steve Biko for the twenty-first century to hold up a mirror of black ability and beauty to see once again the possible and the potential. (2015: 1068, Kindle)

Where do those who, 'being-black-in-the-world', look for self-affirmation and self-validation if not in themselves? The implication of Haffajee's observation is that enfranchised 'blacks' show a tendency to look for change in 'white' people over whom they may not in the short to medium term have total control. The new South African ruling class, asserts Haffajee, 'is no longer white; it is demonstrably black' (2015: 21). Therefore it is located within a majority condition that, in continuing to identify itself as colour-coded, reduces the capacity for agency in social action whose success will render colour irrelevant and at that point affirm the condition of human freedom and dignity.

This tendency on the part of subjects in the imaginary of 'being-black-in-the-world' to diminish or undermine their rising agency also occurs at the same time that another behavioural trend in 'being-white-in-the-world' accentuates Haffajee's concern. Eusebius McKaiser's *Run Racist Run: Journeys into the Heart of Racism* (2015) is a provocative book, written in the context of continuing acts of petty racism emanating from sections of 'white' South Africa which are frequently reflected in the media. McKaiser critiques among other things what he terms 'the myth of white excellence' in the face of their 'unearned privilege of being born into a skin in South Africa' (2015: 134, 142) as an unproclaimed historic benefit, which South African 'whites' have achieved through legislated lack of competition from oppressed 'black' South Africans. McKaiser sets out to explain 'white' South Africans to themselves, through their inability for deep self-critique. Thus, the store of general knowledge that 'black' South Africans had of 'whites' goes beyond the outward manifestations of their power towards the deeper territory of, as it were, explaining 'whites' to themselves. This stance subverts the historical flows of the power of explaining in which 'whites' have assumed 'to know blacks' and were thus able to 'explain' them. This is a radical shift in perspective and signals another part of the shift that Haffajee observed.

Steve Biko has an expression for what is at play here: 'the envisioned self'. 'Blacks,' he writes, 'are out to completely transform the system and to make of it what they wish. Such a major undertaking can only be realised in an atmosphere where people are convinced of the truth inherent in their stand. Liberation therefore, is of paramount importance in the concept of Black Consciousness, for we cannot be conscious of ourselves and yet remain in bondage. We want to attain *the envisioned self* which is a free self' (Biko, 1996: 49, emphasis own). The greatest challenge for South African 'blacks' is to achieve their envisioned self and to invite the entire human condition of the country to participate in it as the new site of human freedom.

The historic transition from 'blackness' to citizen and human is under way, but more work needs to be done to imagine the emergence of the alternative South African human norm in the life to be lived in the future that has to be made out of the changing present. Perhaps the world of the end of 'blackness' is within reach. The thing is to dream it more.

References

Biko, S. (1996) *I Write What I Like: A Selection of His Writings.* Johannesburg: Ravan Press.

Dlamini, J. (2009) *Native Nostalgia.* Johannesburg: Jacana.

Gibson, J.L. (2004) *Overcoming Apartheid: Can Truth Reconcile a Divided Nation?* Cape Town: HSRC Press.

Govender, D. (2016) 'A letter to John Robbie, for Everyone Else Who Heard that 702 Interview', *Daily Vox,* http://www.www.thedailyvox.co.za/letter-john-robbie-everyone-else-heard-702-interview (accessed 15 June 2019)

Haffajee, F. (2015) *What If There Were No Whites in South Africa?* Johannesburg: Pan Macmillan South Africa.

Manganyi, C. (1973) *Being-Black-in-the-World.* Johannesburg: Spro-Cas/Ravan Press. http://www.sahistory.org.za/archive/being-black-world-nc-mangayi (accessed 29 April 2019).

McKaiser, E. (2015) *Run Racist Run: Journeys into the Heart of Racism.* Johannesburg: BookStorm.

Ndebele, N.S. (2007) 'Game Lodges and Leisure Colonialists', in Ndebele, N.S. *Fine Lines from the Box: Further Thoughts about Our Country.* Cape Town: Umuzi, pp. 99–105.

Van Onselen, C. (1996) *The Seed Is Mine: The Life of Cas Maine, a South African Sharecropper 1894–1985.* Oxford: James Currey.

Index

and limitations of studies
on Africans 12
and similarities/differences with
being-black-in-the-world 127
see also entries under 'white'
Biko, Steve xi, 96n4, 140
biological determinism 50
black body, the
as barrier to communication
38, 76
and existential fact of 22, 23
and negative sociological schema
of 7, 22, 37–38, 39, 40, 69–71
see also body, the
Black Consciousness
and concept of freedom 30–31
and emotive quality
of the words 4
and Engelbrecht's views
on 102–103, 103n2
and existential fact of
the black body 22
as expressive of new kind of
responsibility 26–27
as a form of identity politics xv
and importance of liberation 140
and meaning of the words/
concepts 21
and mutuality of knowledge
22, 23, 24, 25, 31
and need for a separatist
posture 31
and perceptions as racialist
20, 24, 31, 45
and re-examination of
relationships 25
and relationship with action 27
as response to white
consciousness (racialism) 24
and the return of the individual
to the community 41
and role of black students 122
as source of inner power 121
as source of political change 89, 91

and temporal dimensions of
23–24, 24–25, 26, 31
see also solidarity
'black pain'
and adjustment in relations
between world views 129
experienced by students 116,
119–120, 120–121, 121
as generalised sense of
oppression 121
see also pain
black people
and achievement of
envisioned self 140–141
and attempts to regain
lost dignity 45
and claims of 'teaching
the world' 6, 132
and consequences of being
conquered 118–119, 137
and designation as 'black' 122
and destruction of
community feeling 41
and distorted relationship with
objects/things 43–44
and evolution of 'black–black'
relationships 129
as 'inferior' under
colonialism 116–117
and limited existential
alternatives 72–73
and ongoing perceptions of
'white' power 138–139
as populations at special
risk 78–79, 138
and post-1994 leadership
role 119
as subordinate component
of SA's spatial system 88,
89, 90–91, 93, 94, 96
and suffering, consciousness
of 23, 25
and suffering, meaning/
source of 63–64

I

identity
  and Black Consciousness xv
  and designation as 'black' 122
  and forging of a common
      identity 129
  and urban Africans 9–10, 11–12
  see also 'us' and 'them' categories
ideological totalism 33–35, 113
illness
  and cultural relativity
      with respect to 59
  as expression of existential
      absurdity 60
  as form of human suffering 58
  and meaning of being ill 58–59, 61
  and ontological interpretation
      of 60–61, 62, 63
Indian people 21, 78
indifference 30, 31
individualism 25, 40, 41, 42, 43
indoctrination 34
industry *see* commerce and industry;
    urbanisation and industrialisation
insecurity 13, 72

L

Langner, T.S. 78
language
  in ideologically totalist
      environments 34
  and use of insulting words 21,
      94
  and use of 'us' and 'them'
      categories 32–33
Leighton, A.H. 78
Leighton, D.C. 78
LeVine, R.A. 46–47
liberalism
  and reactions to Black
      Consciousness 20–21
  and time of deep crisis in xiv
liberation, importance of 140
Lifton, R.J. 33

M

Manganyi, N. Chabani
  and Engelbrecht's comments
      about 'African time'
      100–101
  and influences on xi–xii
  writings of ix–x
  *see also Being-Black-in-the-
      World* (Manganyi)
Mangope, Lucas 89, 89n2
manipulation, in totalist
    environments 34, 35
Matanzima, Kaiser 89, 89n2
materialism 25, 41, 42, 43
Mayer, P. 11, 11n2, 79
McKaiser, Eusebius 140
medicine, traditional vs
    Western 62, 63
mental health
  and integrative status
      of society 77–78
  and public education for 74
  see also community mental health
mental health consultation 82–85
mental health problems
  and association with
      residential settings 13–14
  and integrative status of
      society 6–7, 78–80
  related to dominance of
      white culture 79, 81
  strategies for prevention of 82
  see also African psychiatric
      patients
Michael, S.T. 78
Mignolo, Walter xiv
migrants 12, 61, 62
milieu control 34
Moolman, J.H. 11, 11n1, 88, 95–96
motivation 72–73, 100–101
multinationalism *see* separate
    development (multinationalism)
mutual knowledge
  as consciousness 21

Other Works

Manganyi, N.C. (1973) *Being-Black-in-the-World*. Johannesburg: Spro-Cas/Ravan Press.

Manganyi, N.C. (1977a) *Alienation and the Body in Racist Society: A Study of the Society that Invented Soweto*. New York: NOK Publishers.

Manganyi, N.C. (1977b) *Mashangu's Reverie and Other Essays*. Johannesburg: Ravan Press.

Manganyi, N.C. (1981) *Looking Through the Keyhole: Dissenting Essays on the Black Experience*. Johannesburg: Ravan Press.

Manganyi, N.C. (1983) *Exiles and Homecomings: A Biography of Es'kia Mphahlele*. Johannesburg: Ravan Press.

Manganyi, N.C. (1991) *Treachery and Innocence: Psychology and Racial Difference in South Africa*. Johannesburg: Ravan Press.

Manganyi, N.C. (1996) *A Black Man Called Sekoto*. Johannesburg: Wits University Press.

Manganyi, N.C. (2004a) *Gerard Sekoto: 'I Am an African'*. Johannesburg: Wits University Press.

Manganyi, N.C. (ed.) (2004b) *On Becoming a Democracy: Transition and Transformation in South African Society*. Pretoria: Unisa Press/Leiden: Koninklijke Brill NV.

Manganyi, N.C. (2012) *The Beauty of the Line: Life and Times of Dumile Feni*. Sandton: KMM Review Publishing.

Manganyi, N.C. (2016) *Apartheid and the Making of a Black Psychologist: A Memoir.* Johannesburg: Wits University Press.

Manganyi, N.C. and Attwell, D. (eds.) (2010) *Bury Me at the Marketplace: Es'kia Mphahlele and Company. Letters 1943–2006.* Johannesburg: Wits University Press.

Manganyi, N.C. and Du Toit, A. (eds.) (1990) *Political Violence and the Struggle in South Africa.* Johannesburg: Southern Book Publishers/London: Macmillan.